S0-AXW-089

Great advice that helped ease our family's fears and focused our son on "what needs to happen to finish my senior year." Thanks to the advice outlined in this book, my son is going to a college where he really wants to be, an organization that really wants him there, and many of the little bumps one could experience are already smoothed over. The strategies set forth in the book got us to where we are and the sky continues to be the limit.

— Dr. Jeffrey Allen

At first, the whole college search process seemed overwhelming and raised my self-doubts about whether I was even good enough to apply to my dream schools. This book contains strategies to navigate each stage of the process: choosing schools, how to present yourself, and selecting which college to attend. Thanks to those tips, I was accepted at all my top choices-Harvard, Yale, Princeton, and Stanford- and am currently happily attending Harvard.

— Clarissa Hart, Harvard College undergraduate

This book is a must-read for college-bound students and especially their parents. The authors provide practical advice on how to prepare for the college admissions process—and they debunk many myths surrounding the college search experience. Lum and Soken address head-on the emotional, financial and social realities facing students and their parents on the journey towards college selection. This book will be a useful handbook as we effectively "coach" our daughter through this important life-transition.

— Tom and Kim Pareigat--"Parent-Coaches" of a college-bound HS junior

College-prep books, high school presentations, and college web sites provide a wealth of information for families looking at colleges for the first time, however, this book brought it all together for me, making the college application process less intimidating and more manageable. Lum and Soken share their insights in a conversational style that was accessible and provided me lessons learned and ideas and suggestions that I could apply to my own family's situation.

— Kelly Weyrauch (parent of student accepted to Cornell University)

Help!

Straight Talk for Surviving the College Search

Cheri.

Hope you enjoy the
book

Nelson H. John
4/24/2002

Help!

Straight Talk for Surviving the College Search

Jason Lum JD, MPP
& Nelson Soken Ph.D.

Mill City Press | Minneapolis

Copyright © 2011 by Jason Lum and Nelson Soken.

Mill City Press, Inc.
212 3rd Avenue North, Suite 290
Minneapolis, MN 55401
612.455.2294
www.millcitypublishing.com

All rights reserved. No part of this publication may be
reproduced, stored in a retrieval system, or transmitted, in any
form or by any means, electronic, mechanical, photocopying,
recording, or otherwise, without the prior written permission
of the author.

ISBN-13: 978-1-936780-84-6
LCCN: 2011933749

Printed in the United States of America

Table of Contents

Acknowledgments

Jason:

To my mother, father, and wife, I am humbled and grateful for your sacrifices in ensuring my education would be second to none. Also, my eternal thanks to the universities, organizations, and individuals who awarded me scholarships to make my education possible.

Nelson:

To Leslie, Emmaline, and Evan. Together we navigated this major life transition and became stronger as a family. To Leslie, you are the best partner in life and parenting anyone could have. To Emmaline and Evan, you inspire me to continue to learn. Finally, to my parents and siblings who have always been there with your love, support, and wisdom.

Who We Are

&

Why We Wrote the Book

Jason and Nelson's Story

Take-away:
A little bit about the two of us.

Jason's Story

My journey to becoming a professional college advisor really began in high school in my hometown of Honolulu, Hawaii. My father worked his entire career with the airlines, and my mother stayed at home caring for me and my brother. They never owned a home. At first we lived in a tiny apartment, and then moved into a small house on my grandparents' property. The only real bright spot was that my brother and I went to private Catholic school for thirteen years.

I never stopped to think how my parents paid for the tuition – until I became a senior in high school. I'll never forget seeing my parents' income tax returns when filling out financial aid forms and realizing how much my parents sacrificed for us. I realized then why my father worked multiple jobs to make ends meet and I finally figured out why our ancient Plymouth Reliant hadn't been replaced in twelve years. By all accounts, I had no right to go to private school – let alone think about college.

However, going to college was not negotiable in the Lum household. It was expected, indeed demanded, in my very heavily Asian-influenced household. The problem is that when I reached my junior year in high school, I had very little resources to find my college and, more importantly, how to pay for it.

I also really didn't boast all-star academic credentials. My SAT scores were nothing special and while I got A's and B's, I was hardly the valedictorian.

No one in my family had ever earned a college degree, let alone ever left the Hawaiian Islands to go to the mainland for a degree. However, I'll never forget what my mother told me as I approached the end of my high school career: I deserved to go to the very best schools in the world because I had worked furiously in high school – but paying for this education was my responsibility alone. I could either borrow all the money in the world and pay it all back when I graduated, or I could find others to give me scholarships, grants, and fellowships. I chose the latter.

It was a life-transforming choice. As a senior in high school I made a decision that I would never mire myself in education debt, and that I would get into the very best schools in the United States, regardless. I wasn't sure how I would do it, but I wanted to learn quickly and committed myself to doing plenty of research.

That decision eventually led to degrees from Harvard University, UC Berkeley, and Washington University in St. Louis. It paved the way for me to win a quarter million dollars in scholarship money and gave me the precious gift of graduating debt-free after ten years of post-high school education. My decision created the freedom to choose any job I wanted after graduation and allowed me to live life on my terms without having to worry about meeting the demands of public or private lenders.

When I graduated from law school, I practiced law first with a large multinational law firm, and then served as a civil rights attorney for nearly a decade. However, I realized fairly quickly that my passion lies in working with students and families regarding college education.

What compelled me to give up a lucrative legal career and to become a professional independent college counselor is my unwavering belief that every student in America has a compelling story to tell to colleges and scholarship organizations. What I found in working with young people is that unlocking that story and letting others understand just how special a candidate a student is can lead to unimaginable opportunities. It has also led me into a career where I work with parents across the United States and around the world and speak to Fortune 500 companies and school districts across America.

It also led me to a meeting with Nelson Soken in Maplewood, Minnesota.

Nelson's Story

My purpose for writing this book with Jason is to assist families with their college search and to give them the opportunity to benefit from my family's experience. Why should every family have to start from scratch? Believe it or not, my story begins in Hawaii, like Jason's. I grew up on the Big Island of Hawaii near the town of Hilo. My father worked as a laborer with the local sugar company and my stay-at-home mom took care of the six of us. I am the youngest of six kids, with four older brothers and a sister. Although we did not have a lot of financial resources, my parents provided us with a life rich with love and supported us in all of our endeavors. I remember my parents always sharing with us their view of life in phrases such as *always do your best in whatever you do* and *always remember where you came from.* My parents never had the opportunity to attend college and we were never pressured to go to college, but education was clearly a priority in their eyes and we were encouraged to pursue higher education.

I attended Hilo High School, which is one of the largest public high schools on the Big Island. I did very well in high school, but my SAT scores were around 1000 on a scale of 1600. At the beginning of my college search I did not have a very large search space because none of my siblings and very few friends had ever left the islands and gone to school in the continental United States. Most kids who left the Big Island went to the University of Hawaii at Manoa on the island of Oahu. My only experiences of traveling away from the Big Island had been a few trips to the outer islands and one trip to California when I was ten years old.

4

A defining experience occurred in the fall of my senior year of high school. I was running in the State Cross Country meet in Honolulu and had the opportunity to meet the dean of admissions of Macalester College who was recruiting at Honolulu preparatory high schools (which would not have happened otherwise as I would not have traveled to Oahu just for an admissions interview). I did not have any experience with the admissions process, and it showed. How many students go to their college admissions interview in shorts, t-shirt, and flip-flops soaking wet? Well, I did. The dean of admissions and I sat on a park bench overlooking Waikiki Beach while we talked about Macalester, the Twin Cities of Minneapolis and St. Paul, and the recent twenty inches of snow. This meeting changed my whole perspective on the college search and what was possible. I ended up applying early decision to Macalester and was admitted. Surprisingly, attending Macalester College was cheaper than attending the University of Hawaii at Manoa.

At the end of the summer of 1982, I packed my bags and jumped on a plane to Minneapolis/St. Paul, knowing no one but the dean of admissions. The personal and educational experience transformed my life. I graduated with honors from Macalester with a B.A. in psychology. While at Macalester I worked in the admissions office, giving campus tours. I then went on to get my Ph.D. in child psychology from the Institute of Child Development at the University of Minnesota. I have had the opportunity to work as a teacher, researcher, manager, consultant, and author in academic and corporate environments. My jobs have allowed me to travel extensively and even allowed me to live in Europe for three years with my family. All these experiences would not have been possible without the education I received in those formative years. I can't imagine what I would be like without the experiences in and out of the classroom that shaped me at Macalester.

Fast-forward from 1982 to the present. Education is important to my wife Leslie and me. We have invested a lot of time and money into our two children's education and tried to provide a variety of experiences for our kids, including travels in Europe when we lived there. Leslie home schooled our two kids for years and even started a school with other families to provide an academically rigorous program. When we approached the college search we did it with our own experiences and an open mind. Once we got into it I realized how my background in psychology could be useful to others. One thing I have always appreciated is that logic and knowledge are useful, but when it comes to a decision about your own children and their future during a major parent-child transition period in life, emotion is an enormously powerful driver of the entire experience. This is what motivated our family to meet with Jason. Sometimes an objective outside observer and expert can really help you navigate an important and emotional decision that involves multiple people with different experiences.

My goal in collaborating with Jason on this book is to share some of my family's experience and, given my background in psychology, to provide personal reflections and coping strategies during this important and often stressful time in families' lives. We have successfully navigated the college search process as a family and want to help you in your journey. In my own family's life, we have come full circle as my two children are now attending Macalester, my alma mater, after exploring various options.

Contributors

We would like to recognize and acknowledge the contributions of Emmaline and Evan Soken. The experience of the Soken family to a great extent inspired this book. Emmaline and Evan were involved in the development of the book concept in the early stages and freely shared their thoughts, feelings, and experiences throughout the project. In the Appendix, you will find Emmaline and Evan's advice on the college search and how to navigate the freshmen year of college.

Emmaline

Emmaline is a sophomore at Macalester College. She plans on pursuing a legal career and is currently an English major with a concentration in Human Rights and Humanitarianism. She enjoys writing, reading, photography, and spending time with friends and family. She is happy to be contributing to this book, as she understands the fears and anxiety that go along with searching for colleges. She hopes her experience can ease the process for other students.

Evan

Evan is a sophomore at Macalester College. He is very excited to be declaring a History major. When Evan isn't studying like mad, he enjoys reading, photography, running, and exploring the Twin Cities. He felt strongly about contributing to this book because he remembers well the stressful, overwhelming feeling that can come up in the college search and wanted to do what he could to help streamline that process for as many of his peers as possible.

Fears And Concerns

Fears and Concerns

Take-away:
"Stress is when you wake up screaming and you realize you haven't fallen asleep yet."– Unknown

The stakes are higher in the college admissions lottery these days compared to when we applied to college years ago. You are in a self-selected group of parents with college-bound kids because you decided to read our book. You are wisely collecting as much information from as many different viewpoints as possible. You value education and want to provide your kid the best possible opportunities. You are, in short, being a terrific parent.

At the same time, you are trying not to curl up in a big ball and assume the fetal position when you think about how much a college education costs these days.

The college application process and the idea of paying for college terrify most parents, and for good reason. However, fear often comes from not knowing or imagining the worst possible outcomes. Based on our experience we can imagine the questions swirling through your head:

- How do we even know what schools to consider?
- What schools are good matches for my kid?
- How are we going to pay for college?

- How much of the "work" is my teen's responsibility and how much do I (or *should* I) do?
- My kid is not a 4.0 student and didn't ace the ACT or SAT, so he or she is not going to a "good" school, right?
- If my kid doesn't get into a "dream school" will he or she miss out on career opportunities?
- Can our family navigate this complicated and overwhelming process without fighting and arguing at every turn?

Did we hit the nail on the head? We've both gone through the process personally and professionally. We know what it's like.

Our mission is to reduce your fear and to take the uncertainty out of the college search equation. We'll share our experience and knowledge so you can focus your energy on things that matter. Your time is valuable. We want you to spend it wisely.

In this book we are going to provide you with a toolkit to survive the college search as a family. We will provide information and advice in digestible chunks that you can read when you have time and then apply when the time is right. We will address a wide range of topics such as what the college scene looks like and why it is different now than it was in the past.

We're also going to talk about how your family needs to prepare itself for the search so the experience doesn't turn into a painful one. We hope our advice helps you enjoy the search process.

Then, we will tackle the college admissions process, from organizing yourself, to choosing a college, to applying to colleges. Next, we deal with the issue of money, from applying for financial aid to finding scholarships. Lastly, we provide you with final thoughts on starting the college search, as well as two students' perspectives of the college search and the first year of college. To complete the package, we provide you some of our favorite resources and tell you why we like them so that you can sort through all the information more quickly.

We believe it is important to give our honest and straightforward point of view. We're going to be blunt, and some (or many) of the things we say may be at odds with what your high school tells you. Sometimes you may not agree with what we are saying and that is okay. The point is that you will know where we stand on an issue. Ultimately, you and your teen have to decide what works for you, but at least you will have benefited from hearing a different viewpoint as a starting point.

Let's get started on the journey...

It's Not Your College
Search Experience
Of Years Gone By

It's Not Your College Search Experience of Years Gone By

Take-away:
A surge of kids applying to college over the last few decades has transformed the college search experience. Parents may not recognize the process from when they went through it.

The college search has clearly changed over the years. When we applied to college, our parents were supportive but not as deeply involved in the process as parents are now. Multiple college applications and campus visits to highly selective colleges seemed to be the realm of preparatory school families.

Who could have blamed them? During our parents' working lives, a college degree was neither expected nor required for a vast array of jobs. College was once seen as a playground for the wealthy, privileged, and elite classes. If our parents didn't have the experience to properly guide us in the college application process, it was because they had never thought about college themselves. Many of our parents had an expectation that so long as they finished high school they would be employed by a company that would take care of them for most, if not all of their working lives. Surprisingly, for a good chunk of the twentieth century, that expectation was largely met.

How times have changed.

College applications are breaking records because of a convergence of various factors:

- An ever-growing perception that a college degree is a basic, minimum requirement to succeed in life and to provide job security and higher wages.
- In 2009, the so-called "Baby Boom Echo" (Millennial Generation born between 1980 and 1999) peaked and 3.2 million graduating seniors hit college age.
- Colleges have ramped up their marketing efforts to attract qualified college-bound students.
- Advent of the electronic Common Application has made it easy to apply to multiple colleges at the press of the button.
- Students are applying to a larger number of schools so that they will have the most options for financial assistance and also a sense of safety and security that they will get into desirable schools.
- These trends have created an ever-growing self-perpetuating cycle of stress and turmoil for families. As the number of applications skyrocket, the admissions rate for applicants plummets, which means that next year's students panic and apply to even more schools.

Another issue that arises is that a common pool of applicants vies for the same slots at prestigious colleges and universities. For example, in 2008 Harvard received 27,278 applications, Princeton received 20,118 applications, and the University of Virginia 18,776 applications. In 2010, Johns Hopkins University received 18,150 applications for 1,235 slots in their upcoming freshman class. Closer to home, one of the authors went to Macalester College and the admissions office reports that twenty years ago they would read 2,000 applications per year and by 2008 they were reading over 5,000 applications per year to fill approximately 500 slots in the freshman class.

The stakes are also higher today than they were years ago. It's not the parents' college experience anymore. Choices abound for each student. The implication of this new reality is that family communication and collaboration are critical in the college search. Families need to approach the search as a team and recognize each other's needs. Self-reflection on what matters to the student and family and having common, shared goals are an important foundation for a successful college search. There is no shortage of information, but information without a strategy can become overwhelming. It's a journey that can be exciting and rewarding – or stressful and destructive. Recognizing that the college search process has changed since parents went through it is the first step to getting on the same page both intellectually and emotionally and creating the foundation for a positive experience.

Are you ready to start the adventure? We'll provide you helpful tips on how to navigate the journey both intellectually and emotionally.

Too Few Or An Avalanche
Of Choices: It All Depends

Too Few or an Avalanche of Choices: It All Depends

> ### Take-away:
> *With the college choices available, every student should have no trouble finding good options. The challenge is how to identify the best options for the student weeding through all the choices. Taking the time to plan and sort through the academic and emotional criteria for selection is well worth the effort for the entire family. We are here to help you on your journey!*

Initially, the college selection process may seem easy. Often, families focus on a select group of colleges and universities that are well-known and written up in all the guidebooks and magazines, such as the Princeton Review and U.S. News and World Report. The names that families embrace are Harvard, Princeton, Stanford, Columbia, Yale, MIT, and Berkeley. The fact is that there are approximately 2,500 four-year colleges and universities in the United States and all of them need a new group of freshman each year. In fact, if you include two-year institutions, the number rises to over 4,000 schools. Another growing trend is on-line for-profit educational institutions such as Capella University and Walden University. Our point is that there is no shortage of options for today's college student, and those choices go far beyond what you could imagine or know about before doing some research.

The whole college search experience can swing from too few choices to too many choices. Our advice to you is to not limit yourself to only the schools you have heard of and feel that only those schools can meet the needs of your child. Limiting your options increases stress, as many of the well-known colleges and universities continue to see increased numbers of applications for a small number of slots to fill in their freshman class, which translates into a lower acceptance rate. Remember, there are *thousands* of options. No matter what Johnny and Mary's grades and test scores are like, there are many colleges that are eager to have your child attend their institution. More importantly, there are many schools that can provide your teen with a high-quality educational experience that is life changing.

How could any parent know about thousands of colleges and universities? You can't and you don't need to. Don't get overwhelmed with all the choices. With help, no parent has to know about all the options. With planning, open communication, good research, and advice from professionals, your family can sort through the myriad of options and find the college that suits your child's needs and interests. In the upcoming chapters, our goal is to provide you guidance and advice from our own experiences that will get you on the fast-track to a successful and fulfilling college search experience. We have both been through the undergraduate and graduate school experience firsthand. We will provide you advice from the perspectives of a family who has gone through the experience and a professional who has an impressive track record of getting students into the best U.S. colleges and universities.

Yes, there is an avalanche of choices for colleges, but only a few that really meet your family's, and most importantly, your teen's needs. We will help you identify those hidden jewels.

Information Overload

Take-away:

With the prevalence of information technology and increased marketing to prospective college students, there is no lack of information available. The problem is too much information. Create a strategy for sifting through all the information and learn how to interpret the information through your family's perspective. Sort what matters from what doesn't matter when it comes to the college search.

There is a much-told story in American business schools about consumer behavior at grocery stores. Researchers have found that when consumers have only two or three choices, they make decisions quickly and are confident that they have made the right choice. Yet, when customers see twenty or thirty different choices in the grocery aisle, they are often immediately paralyzed with uncertainty and stand dazed and confused. They don't know how to tell the differences between all those choices! Interestingly, the sheer magnitude of choices often forces customers to walk away, postponing making a choice about what to purchase.

Why do business school students learn this? Because sometimes having too many choices and too much information is worse than having just a handful of resources that you understand and are comfortable with.

Which brings us to the overwhelming quantity of information available about colleges. We put in the search term *college search* into Google and it returned 140,000,000 hits! With greater competition for students and the ease with which students can apply to multiple schools all at once with the Common Application online, the marketing of universities and colleges has greatly increased over the last twenty years. A significant part of the data overload is the access to information via the Internet. Families can now get a wide range of information and opinions about colleges through various sources. There are a variety of guidebooks on universities and colleges that describe and rank them, such as Peterson's, U.S. News and World Report, Fiske Guide to Colleges, College Board, Princeton Review, Colleges that Change Lives, and the Insider's Guide to College. A tsunami of websites provides information, opinions, and advice on colleges, such as Fastweb.com. In fact, it is now possible to get a campus tour without even visiting the campus through http://www.campustours.com/ and http://www.collegiatechoice.com/.

Along with print and online resources, a totally new aid for families has emerged: Independent Educational Consultants. They provide individual families with advice and feedback on college selection, applications, and financial aid. Did we also mention the inevitable appearance of all those parents at school events and friends and family who want to share their experience of the process? What will probably surprise you about the college search is just how much advice is out there.

How do I know the information is up-to-date? How will the

information affect my decisions? Do I even know what I don't know? Where does it end? Most importantly, is the information I am getting accurate? Who should I believe?

As you can probably tell, the problem is not whether or not you have enough information, but rather figuring out whether you have all the "right" information and how to sift through it all. We recommend that you take an active role in the process rather than having information fly at you at light speed and being reactive. The proactive role means that you have created a foundation and strategy for searching for and evaluating the information about colleges and universities. Create a point of view and perspective to funnel and filter information. It's one thing to know that College X ranks higher than College Y, but if you understand what you are looking for then perhaps College Y is the better choice.

In the end, the rankings and views of others are a guide that aids in the search process. But we believe that ultimately the family needs to be the final evaluator of the information. This process will help families sort through the tons of information available and determine what to look for and how to use the information.

Take a deep breath and don't get overwhelmed with all the available information. You don't have to search through all the information. Determine what matters to you. Focus on only the information that supports your family's needs and criteria.

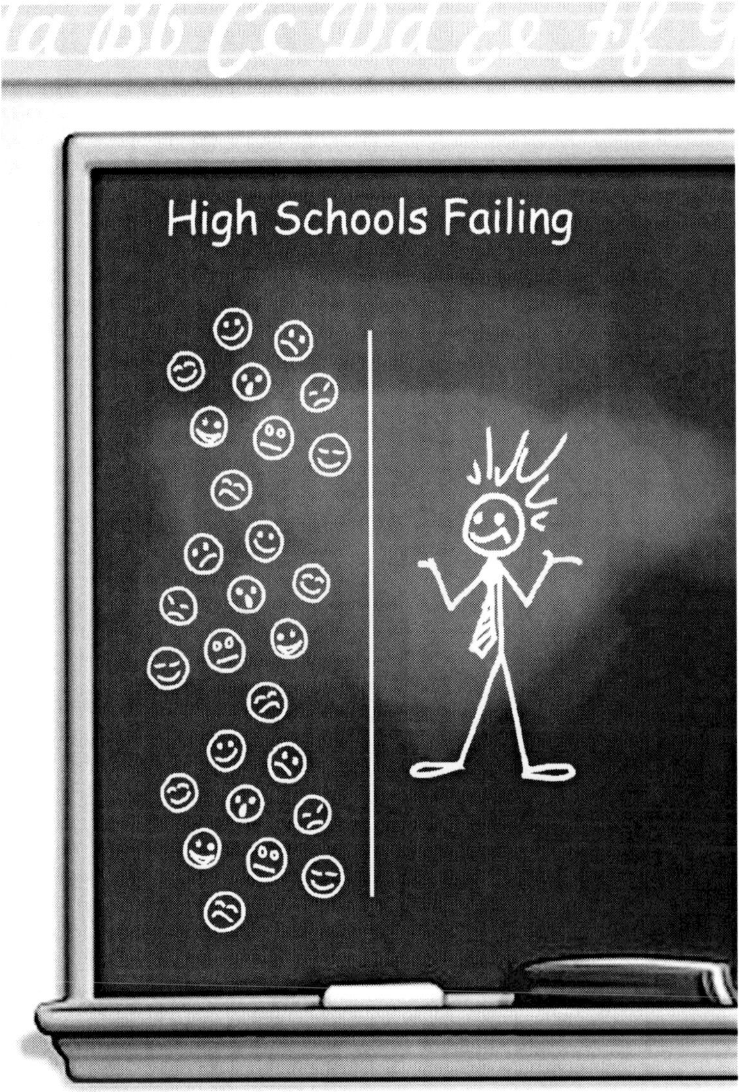
Aa Bb Cc Dd Ee Ff G
High Schools Failing

High Schools Failing

Take-away:

Too many kids assigned to too few counselors, too little funding for college counseling programs – counselors often don't have time to really assess the schools and rely on what they know.

If you ever need evidence of the sad state of college advising today, you should pay a visit to the high school's college counseling office. In fact, we recommend that you do this as soon as possible to understand the challenges that will confront your family as you move forward in the college application process.

Complaints about high school college counseling are legendary: little or no time spent with students; outdated and inaccurate information about colleges gathering dust in the library; short shrift given to both parents and students. In fact, many high schools rely heavily on parent volunteers, and don't require their full-time counselors to visit the schools their students do consider (or should be considering). Most schools don't even begin to work with students regarding college selections until late in the junior year. College recommendations are often made not based upon what is best for the student but rather on which colleges the counselors are familiar with – and that usually means an undue emphasis on local schools.

As bad a job as high schools are doing providing college recommendations, they are failing completely when it comes to educating families about financial aid. In fact, many high schools simply avoid the entire topic of paying for college altogether! High schools sometimes rely on a "Financial Aid Night," which is typically a basic overview of the FAFSA (more on that later) and is almost always inferior to touring the FAFSA website on your own. Families can forget about any substantial and useful advice about scholarships, grants, and fellowships that will help families pay for the escalating cost of college education. And no, a high school simply posting a scholarship opportunity on its website is *not* providing students with good financial aid counseling, in our view.

We know that many counselors defy the odds to help their students – but consider this: even in our home state of Minnesota, there are approximately 800 high school kids for every one high school college counselor (NACAC, 2006). And Minnesota is known for being a state with a strong public education system! In states like California, the ratio is much worse. These numbers scream what many have suspected for a long time, that professional college counseling is not a top priority for school districts and is among the first programs to feel the painful consequences of budget cuts.

We know of families who do not even get an overview or checklist of how they should approach the process of the college search and selection process. One mother told us that she got a checklist from her daughter's school about how the search process should proceed; she and the checklist immediately became very popular with other parents from other schools because they were uninformed about what they should be doing. Copies of the checklist became a hot item among her friends. This type of inconsistency and inadequate assistance is commonplace among America's high schools.

The worst part of the current system is that high schools enjoy a virtual monopoly on providing college information to families. Families, understandably, place a tremendous amount of trust in what their high schools tell them about choosing the right college and how to pay for it. What you don't see behind the scenes is that high schools consistently refuse to allow outside advisors to help them develop their programs to provide better advice to families and students. In fact, our experience (and the experiences of many other professional college advisors) has been that most high schools enforce a blanket refusal with regard to allowing outsiders to work with their students. This is despite the fact that these professionals can provide sound, thoughtful advice and individualized attention for college choices and financial aid – and sometimes offer those services for free.

Remember this sobering thought: your high school college counselor won't lose his job, nor will he get a raise, no matter how your kid does in the college search process. And once your kid graduates, there's a whole group of upperclassmen waiting their turn in line to repeat this cycle. What are you going to do to proactively avoid this situation? We contend that sound college planning does not have to take significant amounts of your time but does take some organization and willingness to seek assistance.

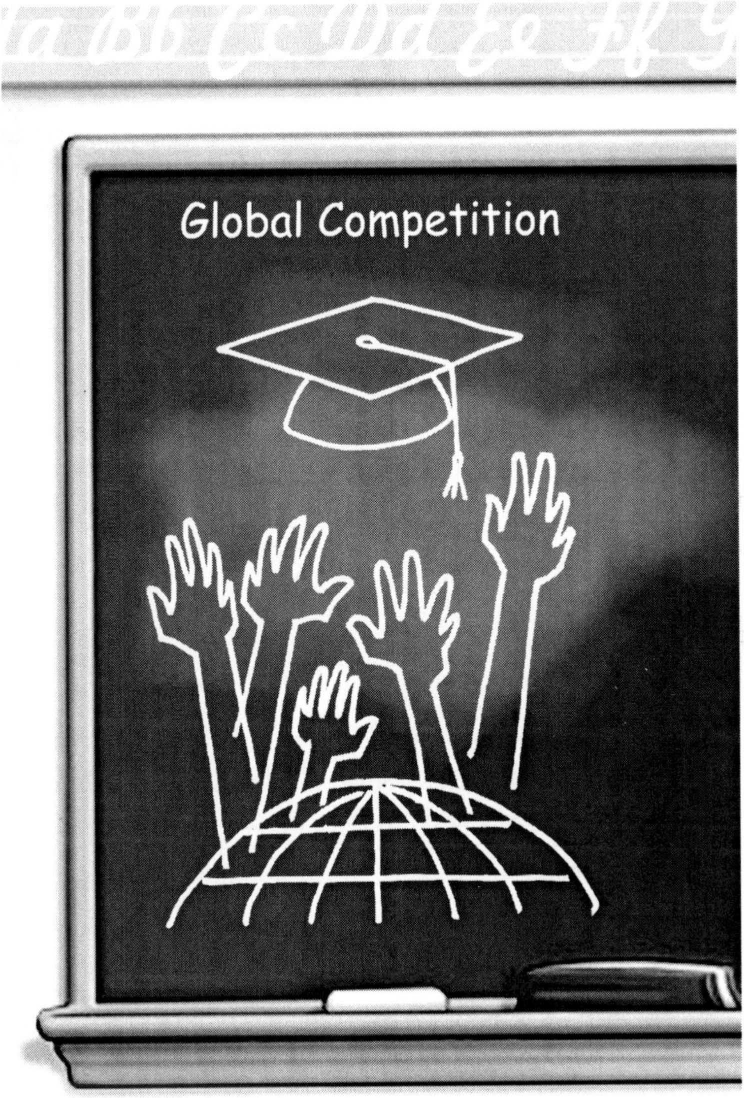
Global Competition

Global Competition

Take-away:
Now American parents are competing with families in Korea, China, and India, making it that much more competitive; it's a different world.

Many families are already aware that Ivy League schools like Harvard and Yale will always attract applications from top American high school students. However, in order to understand college admissions today, some consideration must be given to international students, who are profoundly changing the dynamics of college admission and add yet another unknown to the college search.

Our travels abroad confirm what many already know: American colleges are the world-standard of higher education. In countries such as China and India, an American education is the platinum quality symbol of achievement. Many overseas families spend obscene amounts of money and time to give their children the best opportunity possible to enter America's top educational institutions and quite literally mortgage their livelihoods to make that happen.

To give but one example, many Asian families today send their children to elite East Coast boarding schools where they receive not only a top-notch secondary education, but are also placed in premier college prep programs. These schools give international students a considerable advantage in applying to Ivy League schools and other prestigious American colleges. It is not uncommon for international students to have studied in the United States for at least some of their high school education before attending an American university.

You may wonder: how do these families afford the breathtaking costs of American colleges? What we have learned from our experiences is that the quality and prestige of American college education is so profound that many overseas families will borrow heavily, spend retirement savings, and even rely upon the goodwill of family and friends to ensure that their children have the best opportunity possible to gain admission to an American college or university. Simply put, overseas families see education the way many education-savvy Americans see it – as an investment, not a cost.

What may also shock many American families is the degree to which international applicants are working with professional college advisors. To increase their odds of getting into top colleges and universities in North America, some international applicants pay former admissions officials as much as $30,000 per year for college application advice!

By the way, colleges welcome the rising number of applications of international students for a variety of reasons. First and most importantly, international students are rarely eligible for financial aid, so they often pay the *full cost* of their tuition. For cash-strapped colleges and universities, this is one of the few remaining revenue generators for depleted college bank accounts. Second, many college programs would likely go out of existence without international applicants, including some specializations in science and engineering. Finally, colleges recognize – quite rightly – that international students provide a global learning environment and add a degree of diversity that would otherwise be missing on college campuses.

The surge of interest in American colleges and universities for global applicants is a good thing. It ensures that American college degrees are recognized around the world. More graduates from outside the United States mean more alumni in foreign countries that can help American college graduates find jobs and create business opportunities. International students can also help to provide a more positive image of America when they return home. Silicon Valley would not exist without foreign graduates staying in America, creating jobs and innovating.

But make no mistake about it; the introduction of a new element of competition means that American high school applicants need to present their strongest possible application. Increased competition both at home and abroad means that now more than ever before, good advice, planning, and strategy are key.

Avoiding Family Feuds:
Families Working Together

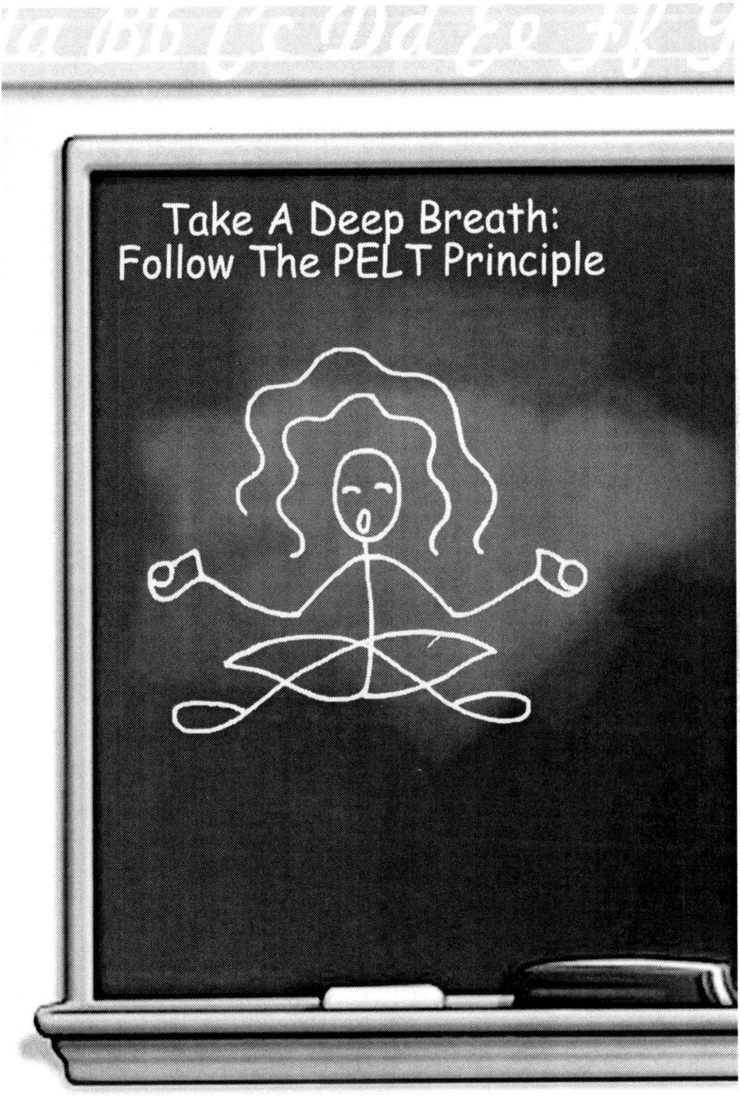
Take A Deep Breath:
Follow The PELT Principle

Take a Deep Breath: Follow the PELT Principle

Take-away:
Learning how to effectively communicate during this major family transition can enrich your relationship for today and the future. Try out the PELT principle: Pause, Empathize, Listen, and then Talk.

Surviving the college search in one piece requires kids and parents to relax at a time of maximum anxiety. The college search is a major milestone toward young adulthood. It's the culmination of years of education, parenting, and growing up, and thus, it's a situation fraught with stress and anticipation for the entire family. You name the emotion and it's probably being experienced during this time by every member of the family. Everyone's emotions are amped up and wired for sound.

Remember the old fire safety rule that you learned as a kid? "Stop, drop, and roll" to extinguish a fire on your clothes or hair? Well, in this case think of it as **PELT**, or **P**ause, **E**mpathize, **L**isten, and then **T**alk so that you can safely remove any conversational sparks that can ignite family relationship fires.

Families that get along during this stressful time figure out the "hot buttons" that get on each other's nerves and lead to triggering conversational landmines. They realize that having lived with each other for years, everyone has developed "rules of engagement" that either nurture each other or cause conflict.

Parents need to recognize that in certain emotional situations, they will behave like a child. Think about times when you are trying to get your high schooler to complete a college application essay or a scholarship on time. The frustration levels rise and the frustrated, emotional child within you overwhelms the mature and controlled grown-up inside. Before you throw a tantrum-filled set of zingers you will regret, take a deep breath and count to ten or send yourself into a time-out. Recognize and empathize with what your teen is going through and try to realize that the road ahead is unknown. They have limited life experience, so you have to be the grown-up.

College-bound teenagers, you can heed the same advice. You are old enough to be self-controlled and mature. Right?

So, as you begin the college search just remember the **PELT** principle when you step into a conversation or situation. Beware of hot button issues that can trigger arguments. These can range from a common phrase such as, "I will do it later" or a common situation such as Johnny sitting back on the couch with his video game controller. When stepping into these situations, be aware that you already have a landmine ready to ignite and explode if not defused. **Step 1**: **Pause** and take a three count (or for some hot buttons, ten count and abandon the situation, even if it means leaving the room) before saying anything. **Step 2**: **Empathize** by taking the perspective of the other person and giving them the benefit of the doubt. Don't assume the worst and also recognize that your teen is stressed out about the search, too, and is trying to cope. **Step 3**: **Listen** to how they are feeling by asking questions rather than telling them how they should feel or behave. **Step 4**: Last but not least, **talk** using positive and encouraging statements and also share how you are feeling. It's about creating a team atmosphere.

Following these simple rules can open things up and create a nurturing family dynamic during this time and make the college search process even – dare we say it? – somewhat enjoyable. Your goal as a family is to balance your stress with the excitement and anticipation of the future. Appreciating and managing each other's expectations is crucial. Good luck and give yourself some slack. You will not always succeed at it, but just recognizing the situation and using these simple rules will improve your family relationship during the search.

Parents' College Experience: It's Not Your Experience, It's Theirs

---

Take-away:

Your experience with college provides you context, but be careful that it does not bias your teen's college search. Remember, times have changed and your student is different than you. Ultimately, it's your child's experience, not yours, but one thing that has not changed is that your teen needs as much emotional support as possible.

Do you remember your own college search? As we reflect on our college searches, what we recall are supportive parents who valued education but did not have a lot of financial resources. Our parents may have had no personal experience with college. They put a lot of the responsibility on us to conduct the search. You may remember a different set of circumstances and experiences. Each of our experiences of high school and post-high school varies greatly because the experience was our own. Many of us went to college right away while some of us took time off.

For many of us, the college years were either right before, during, or soon after the introduction of the Internet. Most of us went through the excruciating exercise of applying to each college with a separate application and essay. College visits and interviews at a large number of colleges across the country were not commonplace. Large numbers of kids didn't jockey for position at the same schools, so rejection rates were not as much of an issue. Most of all, what we have to remember is what has changed since our own college search.

That is our point! Our experiences varied widely because of our family circumstances and what was going on at the time. Avoid the college version of the stories of our youth that our kids tune out: "When I was applying to college we did not have the Internet..."

Don't fall into the trap of overshadowing your high schooler's experience by using your college search experience as the template for your teen. Avoid being self-centered and imposing your own view of the world and/or your own experiences on your kid's experience. Just because you only looked at colleges in your state, doesn't mean your kid has to – or should. Simply because you went to a community college for two years to do your prerequisites doesn't mean your kid has to. You taking the SAT or ACT only once, if at all, doesn't mean your kid should follow in your footsteps. Just because you did not apply to ten schools or do campus visits and interviews doesn't mean your kid should emulate you. Keep the process in perspective. It is the kid's experience, not your experience or our experience; it is *their* experience.

Times have changed and we are all different people, so make sure that you selectively relate your experiences to your family's advantage. Take time to listen, to reflect on your experience, and to appreciate what your child is going through. Recognize your student's personality and strengths. Focus more on what you would have done differently, if you could do it again. Also reflect upon what you wish your parents would have done differently. Focus on how you felt during the process. Understand that over the years you have forgotten a lot of the details and filtered your experience. Hindsight is 20/20.

Remember that your teen has never been through this experience and can only appreciate so much. You have been through this process before but it doesn't have to be the same for your kid. It's a balancing act that can be used to your family's advantage. How the college search works may have changed since you went through it, but one thing that has not changed is that your family is going through a major transition and your teen can use all the emotional support that he or she can get – even if it sometimes doesn't seem that way.

The Best Interests of the Student

> Take-away:
> *It's a balancing act between helping and letting go; it's not easy.*

A typical scene from the 80s and 90s TV sitcom "Married with Children" is Al Bundy sitting on the sofa recounting his days of being a football star back in high school. He constantly relives the days on the gridiron. It seems as though Al spends half of his sad existence looking backwards at his school days wishing he could replay the highlights of his life.

As absurd as Al Bundy's life appears, there are many families in which one or both parents seek to strangely relive their college days through their kids. They unconsciously attempt to live vicariously through their children, hoping to, in essence, experience college all over again. There is nothing inherently wrong with this; parents obviously have a deep and abiding love for their children, and they often see them embodying their hopes, dreams, and aspirations. However, it is one thing for a parent to help a son or daughter in the college search, and an entirely different thing to use a child as a means to achieve dreams, goals, or accolades in college a parent either achieved or failed to achieve.

Jason has often seen parents who arrived at an initial college planning meeting with a list of colleges that their children will be applying to with *little or no input from the son or daughter.* Invariably these are schools that are either (a) firmly in the top fifteen schools in U.S. News & World Report or, (b) are schools that one or both parents attended (or applied to) when they were high school seniors.

This is a dangerous road to travel, not only because it ignores the wants and needs of the child, but also because it almost always leads to one of three outcomes, none of which are good.

When a student attends a school due to strong parental persuasion, more often than not they withdraw from the institution at some point. Sometimes they drop out for good, completely disenchanted with the college experience. Oftentimes they choose to transfer to another institution. Transferring schools might seem to be a relatively minor event in one's collegiate life, but it can be one of the worst things to happen to a college student. It separates the student from friends made during the freshman year, disrupting social networks. It forces the student to learn an entire new university bureaucracy. The worst outcome of all is that the student, out of fear of disappointing the parents, chooses to stay at the school that was unsuitable for them in the first place, racking up mediocre grades and achieving far less than the student would have had the college selection been more appropriate and narrowly-tailored for the needs and desires of the student and not the parent.

It's perfectly fine for a parent to look back at his or her college days and to reminisce about a special fraternity or sorority, athletic achievements on the field, extracurricular accolades off the field, and academic glories. However, there comes a time to turn the page and to allow a teen to move forward with his or her educational journey, and sometimes the best advice is simply to step out of the way and to let the process evolve around the needs, wants, and desires of the child. It's your kid's journey, not yours, but you can help them navigate it and be part of the experience.

Keeping Junior
Close to Home:
Parental View

Keeping Junior Close to Home: Parental View

> Take-away:
> *You need to think about the long-term and also the needs of the kid over time.*

There are few things more difficult than parents watching their son or daughter leave the house to go to college. There is an underlying nagging fear that Junior is leaving the home permanently to build a life of his own. It is scary and sad for virtually all families. In many cases parents try to prevent this from happening by coercing their kids to apply to colleges close to home.

Parents who do this think they are doing the best thing for their children, hoping to provide them with a safety net in case things go wrong, a free Laundromat for their dirty clothes, and a weekend retreat for a home-cooked meal. Some parents even want the kid to live at home for all four years of college. These types of parents are desperately trying to preserve the normalcy that existed in the house for the first eighteen years of their kid's life.

For these types of parents, the college selection process reminds us of what Henry Ford once said: You can buy a car in any color – so long as it's in black. In some cases, it seems a kid can apply to any college – so long as it is local.

However, families that encourage or even require their kids to go to school close to home for these reasons are doing their kids a big disservice with potentially life-damaging consequences.

Consider this: there are approximately 2,500 public and private four-year colleges and universities in the United States. No matter where you live, the number of schools within a one-day driving distance of your home comprises a minute fraction of the colleges in the country. So if your kid is only applying to schools close to home, your family is excluding the *overwhelming majority* of schools in the nation.

You're also probably stunting your kids' maturity if you force them to go to a local college and to live at home. As many college graduates will tell you, the first semester away from home is rough. You may be doing your own laundry for the first time, eating bland dormitory food, and living with a bizarre roommate. (Note: This describes Jason's first semester perfectly, but Nelson was fortunate and had the same roommate for all four years.) But it's a great experience; you're learning to live life with different people, forced to start all over again to make new friends, and frankly learning to be a bit more tolerant of unusual lifestyles and personalities. For many students, this jolts them out of their cocoon in a very abrupt fashion; however, this is preferable to the student remaining in the cocoon. In our view, it is probably one of the most important lessons in college: learning to grow up, be independent, and do things on your own.

If that weren't enough, consider that even if you do keep your kids close to home, the way the economy works today virtually guarantees that your kid will work somewhere other than their hometown. Given the fact that it is highly likely that your son or daughter will work far from home, it makes intuitive sense to instill within your kids a sense of independence, maturity, and self-determination that almost always accompanies going away for college.

Keep in mind that if the very best school for your teen happens to be several miles down the road, then by all means, that school should be included on the college application list. (For instance, Nelson's two kids applied and were accepted to many East Coast schools, but ultimately chose to go to Macalester College, which is thirty minutes from his home, and they both live in the dorms.) But ask yourself honestly, is the primary reason why your kid is applying to local schools because the parents want Junior close to home?

Or have you truly found the very best college or university for your son or daughter in your hometown based upon how that school matches your son or daughter's personality and academic interests?

The answer to that question, and that question alone, should dictate where your son or daughter applies to college.

It's Your Family's Journey: Be Selective with Who and What You Listen To

---

Take-away:

Stop! Keeping up with the Joneses is not the way to survive the college search with your family. It's your journey, embrace it and celebrate the outcome!

The college search is another situation where "keeping up with the Joneses" is not necessarily the right approach. While there is much to learn from other parents who have gone through the experience, it is very easy to get caught up in the excitement and competition of the search. Beware of getting caught up in the outward-focused mentality of *we should do this because it is what all the other families are doing.* Did you hear that Johnny is going to Harvard? What about Mary's full-ride scholarship to Stanford? In the end, who cares about Johnny and Mary's family? It's their experience, not yours.

To keep your family sane, it is important to be grounded. A major trap to avoid is what is called the *confirmation bias*, which is the tendency for people to confirm what they already believe. For example, if you believe that money is an issue and you talk to a friend who says that their kid is going to Stanford at over $50,000 per year, you're probably going to dismiss Stanford as an option. In doing so, you may inadvertently ignore the fact that your friend has told you about the financial aid package that Stanford has given their kid. The trick is to have a strategy regarding who to ask, what information you want and need, and how you interpret that information. Beware of creating obstacles for yourself and particularly only seeking out and interpreting information that fits what you already believe to be true. Be open and be willing (even eager!) to be surprised. Keeping options open as long as possible will serve you and your child well.

Each kid and family situation is different, so make sure you are clear about what matters to you and what your expectations are. Only you know what is best for your family and, most importantly, for your teen. We recommend that you do a self-assessment about your kid, your family, and your current situation. How does your kid deal with new situations and people? What is their learning style? What are their academic interests? What study abroad programs are available? Where is the school located? What is the school's endowment? Once you know what matters to you then asking other people can be useful because you have a family anchor to hang onto as you listen and interpret what others say. Most importantly, you can use outsider information to fill in the gaps of what you know.

In our experience, we found that once we had some ideas about what mattered to our teens, the advice and stories of other families helped us assess how different colleges would meet the needs of our kids. More importantly, it made our family feel more comfortable with our decisions emotionally. Everyone was able to build a picture of how the college experience would be, which made the family transition go much more smoothly. The multitude of data and advice will not make the decision for you, but rather will inform the decision that you have already made.

Don't turn the process into a "keeping up with the Joneses" competition for status. Focus on developing a family mindset based on educational quality, learning, and an emotionally-supportive college environment that is best suited for your family and your teen.

Delegation and Ownership: How to Work Together for the Long Haul?

Take-away:

The college search is one step in the life-long transition to adulthood for students. It is also a major transition for parents in letting go. Working together is a crucial part of life education.

The college search is part of the ongoing educational process for your teen. The ancient Chinese strategist Sun Tzu once famously noted, "Every battle is won before it is ever fought." The same attitude applies to the question of how to get through the college search as a family. Planning ahead can make a critical difference in winning the short-term battle of getting your kid into the best college. At the same time, planning helps you win the war of using the college search as a stepping stone for your kid's continued growth toward independence and adulthood. A key question is how to maintain civil family relationships while achieving these short- and long-term goals for your kid.

Everyone embarks upon the college search with different fears, questions, and expectations, and therefore it's essential to have a game plan. By carefully identifying what you know, what you don't know, and how to achieve measurable objectives, you avoid turning this conversation into an emotional meltdown, where a "discussion" dissolves into an endless argument and everyone walks away more upset and apprehensive.

A major success factor in the college search process is creating a game plan around who is responsible for what aspect of the college search. There is a fine line in determining your role as a parent and the expectations you have of your college-bound teenager. The first thing is to assess the current state of your relationship and expectations. You can't just suddenly ramp up your expectations and make your teenager accountable for everything if that is not the way life has been so far. Every family has to draw their own proverbial "line in the sand" concerning their expectations and accountability for each other, taking the past into account.

In general, the key premise to start with is to avoid commandeering the process. We believe that parents should partner with their teen to help where necessary in areas where the student lacks familiarity. So, how does a family create a game plan for sharing responsibility for the college search? Some tips to consider include:

- Continually be encouraging and show your teenager that you believe in them and that the college search process is ultimately owned by them.
- Don't do for your student what they are capable of doing on their own and allow them to demonstrate their independence and abilities.
- Have your child take responsibility for their part of the college

application.

- Take responsibility for areas that only you as a parent know about, but share the information and your perspective as much as possible so the student is informed about what is happening and has a realistic view of the situation.
- Be patient and supportive and keep communication lines open.
- Given these family transitions, anticipate emotional situations during the process.
- Treat your teen like an intelligent and capable individual.
- Be open to assisting your student where necessary, but be careful not to take over the process or to turn into a "nag" that continually bugs your child. Ultimately, it is their process, so they should be accountable and learn that there are consequences. It's like going back to when they were young children in terms of rewards, punishments, and consequences for their behavior.
- Develop mutual expectations and agreements for the college search and beyond so that you can avoid misunderstandings.

With everyone given discrete roles in the process, everyone is a vital and thriving member of a team tackling the college search. Ultimately, everyone needs to feel like part of the team and to have "skin in the game." This is an opportunity for parents to transfer more responsibility to their student so that the student can be more independent. Think of the college search as part of your teen's educational journey toward adulthood and – just as importantly – as the beginning of the healthy parental process of letting go of your child.

Leading Versus Managing: The Transition to Your Kid's Independence

Take-away:
"You do not lead by hitting people over the head. That's assault, not leadership." – *Dwight D. Eisenhower*

As your family proceeds with the college search process, it is important to think about the proper parental role. Something to keep in mind in this important transition period is the distinction between a manager and a leader. Remember that you are in the midst of a major family transition during the college search. This is a time when your child is preparing to leave the nest and spread his or her wings in ways that they have not done before.

A manager is responsible for getting the job done and directs and controls who and how the work gets done. A leader focuses on people and inspires others to follow him or her because of their vision. Leaders capture the heart of people and get them excited about doing what needs to be done to achieve the goal.

Let's bring this back to the college search. As you think of your role as a parent during this time, start to make the transition from manager to leader. A manager parent would focus their energy on directing, controlling, planning, organizing, and scheduling their people, namely the child, to finish the work and use whatever means necessary to get it done. Managers are transactional and the goal is to get the work done in the short term. The leader parent would focus on the child's needs and figure out how to create a team atmosphere that raises morale and empowers the kid to want to do the work. This type of atmosphere would create positive energy and a desire for all involved to play their role in getting the work done but not at a high emotional cost. The leader parent also creates the vision of why it is important for the kid to get the work done and how it contributes to their future.

So what we are asking you to think about is how you as a parent can set the direction and climate for your family. Being a leader rather than a manager does not mean you will not help set schedules and deadlines and/or communicate expectations. It just means that your focus will include how the context and situation affects the student and the rest of the family along with getting the job done. It also means that the short-term tasks don't overshadow the long-term relationships and outcomes that you are trying to achieve.

Keep in mind that the goal is selecting a college that will suit the needs of your teen as well as preparing them emotionally and interpersonally to succeed. Don't lose the forest for the trees. There are life lessons to be learned in the entire process, one of which is to learn how to deal with stressful situations and succeed.

Are you ready to lead your family through this transition? Set a long-term vision and direction that keeps everyone's eyes on the prize. Inspire your family, particularly the student, so you create followers of the vision and a sense of loyalty. Lead quietly with a steady hand that encourages and supports, rather than with coercive and heavy-handed management.

Organizing for Success

Eliminate Distractions

Take-away:
Time is short so ignore activities that don't add value to you or your college application.

The world around us seems to devour our time. It seems that distractions are everywhere and new ones seem to pop up every day.

As bad as it is for parents, our kids seem to be inundated with even more distractions between activities and technology. In fact, parents are contributing to the situation by transforming themselves into chauffeurs, shuttling their children from soccer practice to dance class to karate instruction to violin lessons. When asked to explain this busy lifestyle, many parents reply that this is the best way to get their kids ready for life and for the college application process. Let's not waste time, they say – as they race off to another practice with their kids.

You shouldn't waste time, but an addiction to overscheduling is neither healthy nor productive.

Let's start off with the biggest distracter imaginable – a part-time job. We have heard from countless families that a student holding a part-time job is someone who is more mature, better able to handle money, and will ultimately be a more responsible individual. This may be true for many teens. But we take a different view of students working during school. First, in Jason's many years of advising some of the top students in the nation, it has been extremely *rare* for those students to be working part-time jobs. For these families, part-time jobs would have been the ultimate time waster. When you're spending ten or twenty hours a week earning minimum wage scooping ice cream or mopping floors, think about what you are not doing. You are likely not participating in activities that can add real value to your college application. You are not volunteering for a local soup kitchen. You are probably not applying for scholarships because frankly you don't have enough time. We know many families would argue that you can work and do all of the above at the same time, and we would agree. However, we would suggest that most teens can't do everything perfectly with an enormous load of commitments, and we all have only twenty-four hours in a day.

Think of it this way: for the ten bucks or so you make working at your local convenience store or gas station, you may be limiting your time and ability to research colleges and to apply for scholarships. That could have a much greater long-term impact on your earnings potential and on your personal satisfaction. We know there are many kids out there that don't come from wealthy families (ours included!), but ask yourself honestly: is your son or daughter working a part-time job because of dire financial straits or because Johnny or Caitlin wants to purchase a used car? Is the money being earned by the job going to a good purpose? What could the student be doing with the time spent on the job if he or she decided not to work?

Let's focus on another commitment that tends to be a time waster – sports. Now don't get us wrong. If you love basketball, football, or tennis, we're not going to convince you to give up something that you really enjoy. If you're a star athlete with a 4.0 GPA, great SAT scores, and lots of volunteering and activities, then more power to you; don't change a thing! However let's be honest. Sports demand extreme time commitments from students. We think it is unfortunately very rare to find a perfect student athlete; if you are deeply involved in athletics, you're probably taking away time for your studies, volunteering, and college planning. Teens should ask themselves: Are the countless hours you are spending on athletics taking away time from other activities and are you losing focus on the long-term endeavor of finding and getting into the college of your choice?

Sometimes students and parents feel that time spent on sports is a good investment. They feel that colleges will admire the ability of the student to balance athletics and academics. Families might even feel that their son or daughter will win a sports scholarship. Call us pessimistic, but our experience is that very few students are ever going to win a scholarship based purely on their sports potential, unless you're the next Tom Brady or Michael Jordan. Even if you do win a sports scholarship, the college will get its money's worth – once you arrive at college you will be expected to invest even more time in your sport of choice. If the only reason a teen is involved in sports is because his or her family thinks it will help in the college application process, the family may be prioritizing incorrectly, and might be overlooking other activities, such as volunteering, which may add more value to the college application.

Finally, the most egregious time wasters are video games, television, and computer games. We've seen too many families tolerating a son or daughter spending countless hours on Xbox 360 or Sony PlayStation. If you're spending eight hours a day watching television, then your priorities are completely off the mark. And while obviously the Internet is an important vehicle for research and homework, if you are planted in front of your computer playing World of Warcraft or friending your 1,000th buddy on Facebook, then you need to take a step back and ask: what am I doing, why am I doing this, and – most importantly – is my competition for college wasting their time to the same degree? Answer: they are not.

Keep in mind that you can do all the above in *moderation* and still be an extremely successful applicant for colleges and scholarships. You can enjoy sports, you can accept a part-time job during the summer, and of course you can enjoy playing computer games (and even "friend" us on your Facebook account!). The point here is moderation – and being a ferocious prioritizer especially as you near the time you apply for colleges and scholarships.

When to Begin? Start Early in High School

Take-away:
College admissions start way before your senior year!

The college admissions process is probably the first major event in your kid's journey to adulthood. It's your teen's first experience with the concepts of *career planning* and a *resume*.

Parents need to help their kids realize that they need to figure out what their long-term aspirations, interests, and views are early in their high school years, if not sooner. The reason is that the college admissions process has gotten so much more competitive in recent years that you really can't start too early.

Finding the colleges that meet the needs of your kid requires dedication, focus, and commitment to the journey both from them and you as parents. Make no mistake; ultimately, it's the student's responsibility. Students have to make choices with their time. Is it short-term gratification spending all their time with friends, television, and video games? Or is it taking some of their time planning for the future? It's always a balance between the short- and long-term, but neglecting the long-term has consequences.

Rome was not built in a day and a superior college application can't be built in a year. More importantly, a teenager growing into a well-functioning adult is not built in a year. Building a top-caliber college application and creating a terrific all-around record for your kid takes time.

What are the colleges looking for? What will the admissions staff think of your child after reading all the materials the he or she has put together for the application? It's about creating a consistent and holistic picture for the admissions staff. First and foremost, it's the quality of the student's academic record. But it's not just the grades; it is the quality of course work. Is it an easy "A" or is it a quality "B" in an AP course? Is there a consistent record of always taking the toughest courses available? It doesn't hurt if the student's standardized test scores are also good – but more on that later. Consistent academic performance and test scores are the most important components of a college application – but they are just the beginning.

Rounding out a consistent and persuasive college resume requires a commitment by students who invest in experiences that matter to them. College admissions offices can pick out applicants who pad their resume but do not invest in learning from their experiences. What activities do they invest in, and have they done it for extended periods of time? What skills have they cultivated and crafted? Is what they have done reflected in their portfolio and/or college interviews? Are they interesting people beyond the grades and test scores? Does the student know him or herself and would they uniquely and actively contribute to the campus?

Ultimately, getting to the point of impressing the college admissions staff and, more importantly, developing as a person requires a student to start on their college resume early and demands motivation in investing in self-exploration. This does not require teens to reinvent themselves, but it does demand an early start to build a winning application.

Don't Work Just with Your HS College Counselor

Take-away:
Your counselor should not be your sole source of college information.

California has long been the American dream – a land of breathtaking bridges, glamorous Hollywood, and romantic wineries. It is also in America's Golden State where you will find one of the most harrowing ratios in the country: 990 to 1. That is the number of students per every high school college counselor in California's public high schools. In case you're wondering, virtually every state in the nation has ratios shockingly similar to California's.

How did we reach this point? Simply put, America is failing to put its money where its mouth is when it comes to college counseling. For all the talk from school boards and high schools about prioritizing college prep, when it comes time for students to apply to college, most schools don't have enough counselors to work with the kids. Like everyone else, college counselors only have twenty-four hours in a day, and most of their intensive work with college-bound seniors happens between September and December. With the astonishingly high ratio of teens per college counselor, is it any wonder why many high schools are unable to provide teens with the specialized attention they deserve when applying for college?

Let's also be clear here; we think that high school college counselors do as much as they can with limited resources. They are almost uniformly underappreciated, and are expected to help all seniors – from underachievers to 4.0 students – get into college or some post-high school career-oriented program. They work nine months a year in understaffed and under-appreciated offices. Few employees in public education are asked to do so much with so little resources.

If you don't believe us, look at the numbers. Virtually every state has severely cut their education budgets. There is no money to speak of to send high school college counselors on nationwide tours of colleges and universities to talk to college kids, find out about curricula, and to explore little-known facts about important regional and national colleges. The money is not there to aid high school college counselors to be at the cutting-edge of their profession.

Simply put, if you are relying only on your high school college counselor, you are not doing enough to succeed at the college selection and application process. We are categorically **not** saying you should stop working with your high school counselor – actually, quite the opposite. Students should work with their college counselor, utilize whatever resources are in the counseling office, and of course learn what the office can do for them. But in terms of individualized attention and tailor-made preparation for the colleges best suited for the student, there are many other things you can do – described in this book -- than relying on an overburdened and under-financed college counseling office at your kid's high school. You need to take a proactive approach early in the process and look at the college search as an investment in your kid's future. Just don't expect your high school to do all the work for you.

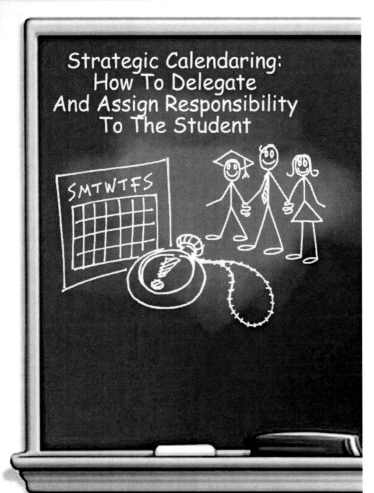

Strategic Calendaring: How to Delegate and Assign Responsibility to the Student

Take-away:

"You may delay, but time will not." – Benjamin Franklin

Getting through the college application process in one piece takes planning. Checklists for planning the college search abound. A quick search of Google with the search term "college application checklist" yields a lot of checklists from reputable sources such as the College Board and American Education Services as well as educational consultants and authors. These checklists provide good advice, schedules, and proposed calendars.

Checklists and guidance are not the problem. The challenge is to get students to stay focused and motivated to get the work done. It is about execution.

How do you delegate to your student and set them up for success if they don't invest time into the process? Our primary recommendation is to do everything possible to stay ahead of the game. Strategically set up a schedule and calendar that builds in a lot of buffers by creating personal application deadlines months in advance of the real deadlines set by the colleges. Because as a Spanish proverb says, "Tomorrow is often the busiest day of the week."

So how do you make it happen? You know your teenager better than anyone else (despite what your teenager might think).

Figure them out. What makes them tick? Is your kid normally a procrastinator? Do high levels of stress and anxiety lead to their being overwhelmed and avoiding getting things done? Is your kid a perfectionist? Is your kid easily distracted? Does your teen fall into the trap of being paralyzed with guilt when they don't hit deadlines? Figure out what stops your kid from getting things done and help them get over the challenge while he or she tries to get through and enjoy their high school years.

Motivate them. Help them realize that putting off working on the application has so much more downside than upside. Putting the college search off for whatever reasons leads to greater stress, more family discord, and the potential for missed opportunities. A haphazard college selection process means not finding a college that best fits your student's needs. Waiting means not visiting and investigating schools to see what they are really like. Waiting too long before your teenager works on their college essay means that they won't have time to get feedback, which usually translates into a poorly-written essay. Procrastination guarantees your student will not get the best people to be recommenders and those recommenders probably won't have as much time to write a great recommendation. Let's face it, waiting translates into less time to deal with the unexpected and prevents presenting the high school record in the best possible light. It also means added stress and a greater probability of not succeeding at finding the best place to attend college.

Some words of wisdom for your student from our own experiences in getting the job done:

- Create a vision of the outcome so there is something to look forward to at the end of the journey.
- Get started early and assess what needs to happen.
- Make a plan and set goals.
- Take on small pieces so progress is continually made – it will feel great to see real progress.
- Schedule dedicated time to make progress and avoid distractions.
- Stay motivated by getting someone to report to. In our case, it was Jason as a third party.
- Just get started, even if it is not perfect. As Dawson Trotman once said, "The greatest amount of wasted time is the time not getting started."
- Be reasonable and don't allow them to beat up on themselves and, as parents, don't beat up on them.
- Try to keep it fun by creating a game out of it.
- Celebrate early and often along the way to maintain motivation.
- Keep positive energy high and negative energy low by communicating often along the way.
- Finally, build in a lot of buffers so that there is ample time to get it done without stress. These buffers take into account the surprises of life.

Your family can do it. Focus on the prize and set yourself up for success.

Start Benchmarking Dates

Take-away:
*Use a written planner and plot key dates (e.g., FAFSA,
application to State U.) as early as possible.*

Stephen R. Covey, the author of *The 7 Habits of Highly Effective People*,
is one of the world's most beloved self-help experts. He is also a
favorite author of ours. Among the many tips that Covey shares, one
is extremely important: plan ahead and use a written planner.

Sounds simple, doesn't it? Incredibly, it is the most useful strategy
for completing successful applications.

We realize that we live in a day of iPads, BlackBerries, PDAs, and
Microsoft Outlook. We use these ourselves. But we can't think of
a *worse* way to plan ahead for the college road than to rely solely
on these electronic gizmos. It is crucial to know about application
deadlines so you can scare yourself into action. The beauty of a
written planner is that a student can visually determine what is
coming up this week, next week, and next month. It provides a sense
of urgency that a day-by-day electronic calendar, a neat iPad app, or
a reminder pop-up on Outlook could never do. Sometimes it's good
to *see* a deadline to steer you into action.

In fact, one idea that has worked exceedingly well for many savvy students is to buy a wall calendar from a local office supply store, then circle important dates with a wax marker. We recommend using different colors to circle when different applications are due. You might choose red for college applications and green for scholarship deadlines. Check off those circles when you've completed that task. That gives you a justified sense of progress in what you are doing. Keep in mind that especially with scholarships, the deadlines fall all over the map and are not simply competitions where you submit applications in the spring.

Here's the key: you need to have two sets of deadlines. The first set of deadlines includes the deadlines imposed by the colleges, universities, or scholarship committees. Those are the non-negotiable "drop dead" deadlines – if you don't get your materials in by that date, they simply will not be accepted. One note to the wise: if you think that colleges or scholarship organizations are flexible regarding their due dates – well, you are in for a very rude awakening. They will literally throw away your application if you are even a day late.

Your other set of deadlines is far more important. They are *your* deadlines. You should ideally set your deadlines for any given application at least one month prior to when they are due.

Why should you do this?

Because it allows you to have a buffer in case emergencies arise. People get sick. You might fall in love. Parents may have to unexpectedly move for work. Life happens. Because of that you cannot neatly predict every event to happen between now and application due dates. So set your deadline at least one month prior to the college or scholarship deadline. When you set personal deadlines well ahead of the actual deadline, you don't have to live a life of nerve-rattling anxiety, wondering if the teacher wrote your recommendation letter on time, or whether or not your transcripts were sent in a timely fashion. Because you've given yourself a buffer zone, you can rest easier.

Organization is one of the most important features of successful applicants. By following just the few simple rules noted above, you will put yourself ahead of the vast majority of your classmates and will have an edge regarding scholarship and college applications.

Be A Hawk:
Grades And Academics

Be a Hawk: Grades and Academics

> Take-away:
> *The student's number one priority that trumps all else: GPA.*

There are certain things that a student can control and things that a student cannot control. A student cannot control precisely what a teacher will write in his or her letter of recommendation. Teens really can't predetermine their standardized test scores. But students have absolute control over the most important part of any application.

Grades.

We believe that grades are so vitally important that absolutely *nothing* you do should interfere with your attainment of a high GPA. That includes sports, part-time jobs, and over-committing to volunteering. We wouldn't be making this sort of sweeping statement unless we felt that this is the single most important part of your application and that you largely have complete control over the outcome.

We know that many parents worked during high school and want their children to also work to appreciate the value of money. That's a worthwhile belief. We also know that many parents encourage their students to be active in sports to learn the lessons that only teamwork can impart upon a young person. Again, we agree with embracing teamwork. But if a student is suffering grade-wise because they are devoting their time to the varsity track team, or working fifteen to twenty hours a week at a local convenience store, or over-extending him or herself on pet projects or hobbies, then that student needs to stop what they're doing and focus on grades.

In addition, for teens that are looking to gain admittance into America's premier colleges and universities, it is not nearly enough to score high grades. The student also needs to ensure that the quality of the courses they're taking demonstrates a serious commitment to academics. Preferably, by the time they reach their junior and senior year, there will be lots of AP and honors courses on their transcript.

However, if these courses are resulting in a much lower GPA for your son or daughter, then it is far better for them to be taking a non-AP course and getting a higher grade. Many high schools will tell you the opposite, because they believe that students should be challenging themselves to the strongest extent possible, even if it results in a somewhat lower grade. While there's no arguing that AP and honors courses are more challenging, if you are taking these classes and not doing well academically, there is not a single elite college in the world that is going to consider those grades in a positive light. They will, however, take immediate note of a superb GPA.

Simply think of your GPA as a fortress. Protect it at all costs, and let absolutely nothing interfere with your laser-like focus on attaining a high GPA. If you're getting good grades, and playing sports, holding a part-time job, and are deeply involved in many other things outside of school, then don't change a thing you are doing. But if you are honestly suffering from a lower GPA because of other things in your life or at school, it's time to reevaluate things right <u>now</u>. Remember, your grades are your calling card, and they're the most important part of how the admissions staff sees you.

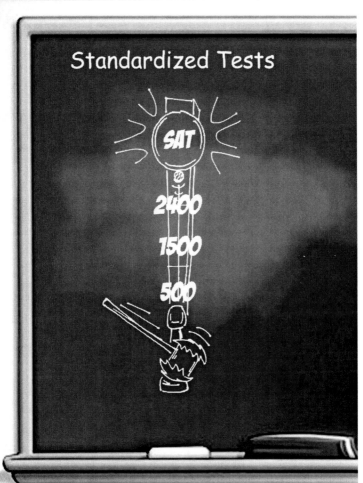

Standardized Tests

Take-away:

Understand which one to take, its importance, and how many times to take it, etc.

Next to grades, there is nothing that strikes fear into the hearts of students more than two three-letter words: ACT and SAT. These two standardized exams continue to terrorize legions of high school students, who grossly overestimate their importance for college admissions. An entire industry has developed not only in offering these tests but also in coaching students to take them.

These tests are important, but are not the sole factor in admissions decisions. In fact, we feel that not only should most students *not* worry too much about these tests, but that the more that they know, the less they would be intimidated by these tests.

First, let's talk about which test you should take. The ACT is taken primarily in the Midwest, and the SAT is taken everywhere else. This has nothing to do with what the colleges need. In fact, most colleges will take either test. The reason why Midwesterners take the ACT is because the ACT was developed in Iowa, and the SAT is based out of the Northeast. That's it. It's purely a matter of geography. So take your pick of which test to take – the colleges don't care.

The next question is which test would be best for my child to take. Unfortunately, there's no easy answer to this question. They are two very different exams. The most obvious difference is that the ACT has a "science" section and the SAT does not. Strangely, the ACT "science" exam doesn't really test your knowledge of science, but rather the questions are simply based on a science fact pattern. Therefore, if you get straight A's in your science classes, it does not mean that you are going to ace the ACT science section.

The only real way a student can figure out which exam is a better fit is to simply take both exams at home by purchasing a book that contains old versions of the real exams. There is some anecdotal evidence that the SAT is a more coachable exam, but this is purely speculative because each student tests differently. There is simply no alternative to taking both exams under timed conditions at home to see which test is better for a student.

Many teens mistakenly think that they should take these exams as soon as possible so that they can retake them if they need to. The folks at SAT and ACT have a great business model: they magnanimously allow you to take the exams as often as you like, and you can send the highest score to the colleges. It's just a coincidence that the ACT and SAT folks pocket millions annually from students who retake these exams three or four times. Pure coincidence.

This might sound like a great thing, but it really is an awful idea. Why? It reinforces student anxiety about their test scores and encourages them to take and retake these exams to the point of sheer ridiculousness.

The best thing that students can do is to wait as late as possible in the junior year to take one of these exams. Go into the exam room thinking that this is the one and only time you'll take it. Don't fall back on the thinking that you can retake the exam; taking any of these exams is a taxing process and you really don't want to be taking these pressure-inducing exams more than twice, in our view.

Also, keep things in perspective; if you are scoring in the 80th or 90th percentile on either exam, that means that eight or nine of every ten students scored worse than you did. That is an outstanding score for every college in the United States. Retaking the exam after scoring relatively high is simply imposing time and emotional burdens upon a student that will inevitably take away from studies, scholarship applications, and volunteer work. Remember that your time is your most valuable asset, and there's little need to devote more time to standardized tests if you're already scoring at a fairly high level.

We're also not entirely sold on the idea that you need to purchase expensive coaching programs from outfits like Kaplan and Princeton Review. We've met many students who have taken these thousand dollar prep classes, and few have scored spectacularly better, if at all, on the SAT or ACT. We believe that there is no substitute for simply sitting at home under timed conditions and taking old versions of these exams. Therefore, no preparatory class is going to substitute for the time and effort you employ taking practice exams. In fact, Kaplan and Princeton Review rely heavily upon making you take these tests under timed conditions – so why not do it yourself and save some money?

Perhaps we are in a minority on the subject, but we happen to believe that there are some kids out there who simply take these tests very well, and some students who don't. These are *not* intelligence tests. They have no real predictive power about your ability to do well in college. They simply test your ability to take the SAT or the ACT.

Here's the best news of all: of all the trends we have seen in recent years for college admissions, perhaps the most prominent is the de-emphasis of standardized tests in the admissions process. In fact, there are many great colleges and universities in the United States that either make these tests optional or don't require them at all. They are but one factor in a very complex process, and even if you don't do terribly well on these tests, it is certainly not a mark against your intelligence and will probably have little impact ultimately on your college application experience.

Assembling The Portfolio

Assembling the Portfolio

Take-away:
You've got one chance to make a first impression.

Your teen has worked his/her tail off for years compiling a superior personal and academic record. Now what? It's time to put it together and send it off.

Word of warning: it's nearing the end of the race and attention and focus are critical. All the hard work can go down the drain if not managed well.

Marketing matters. Honestly marketing what you have done to your various colleges of choice is important. As the saying goes, you only have one chance to make a first impression. Take the time to put together a compelling case for each of the colleges. One size does not necessarily fit all. Your student has the raw material, but it requires additional work to customize for each college. It's about your child marketing his or herself to the colleges. Marketing does not mean copying and pasting from one application to another – it means making a connection between the student and a unique college based on what each can do for one another.

Timing matters. A critical part of the application is your teen's recommendations. It's their references who have an opportunity to give an independent assessment of who they are as people, what they have done, and their potential for college success. If potential advocates are not contacted early enough and/or not given enough time, the outcome can be disastrous. They may not have time to do a recommendation. Nothing irritates a high school teacher more than being given just days to complete a letter, and can you really blame them? After all, why should they suffer for a student's procrastination? Worst yet, they may create a generic "Dear John" letter that does not differentiate your student from the other thousands of form letters that admissions officers read.

Quality matters. Admissions officers are overwhelmed with applications to read, so the little things matter a lot. Avoid typos or poorly written work – it will stand out for the wrong reasons. Make sure someone edits materials. It constantly astonishes us just how many college essays never go through a second or third draft, let alone are never proofread by others. This is a sure-fire way to ruin your application, especially if you are applying to selective colleges.

Completeness matters. Double check to make sure everything is in. Missing an opportunity because of a stupid mistake would be catastrophic. From the college's perspective, you are forecasting what you would be like as a student – if you don't pay attention to the details, you signal that you probably won't care too much for studying.

Sweat the details. Your teen and probably you have worked too hard to blow it at the end.

Come up with a system or get help so you ensure the best quality work possible.

Hire a Private Counselor

Take-away:

College is a major investment in your kid's future. So why not invest in it? If you're purchasing or selling your house don't you typically get expert assistance? Do the same with college admissions and consider a private counselor.

Paying for college is the largest expense in your lifetime next to buying a home. You have invested most of your adult life into bringing up your child. Don't stop focusing on them as they are about to launch into the next phase of their lives. Be a savvy and active college consumer.

As with many things these days, the college search seems to sneak up on families and appears to last forever. Information abounds but guidance in walking through the process can be scant and spotty at best. Resources at many high schools are strained, and therefore depending on high school counselors for college admissions support may not be enough. We strongly recommend considering seeking outside assistance.

As we discussed at the beginning of the book, there is no shortage of information and advice from multiple sources. In fact, the Internet has led to the opposite problem – too much information. So how should you tackle the process without getting overwhelmed? How do you support the student in the process while allowing them to take more control and accountability for getting things done? Where do you get up-to-date and comprehensive guidance on selecting a school that fits your student's interests and personality? Can you get feedback on their application that is both objective and based on knowledge of what colleges are looking for today? Perhaps most importantly, just how do you maintain positive family relationships during this major life transition?

Here's one way to solve it: get a professional to work with you. Organizations like the IECA (www.educationalconsulting.org) list private college counselors who need to prove they have the background and have made the site visits necessary for membership. Their members must sign ethical statements upholding professional standards. When you hire a private consultant, you will get personal advice and attention, detailed college lists with explanations for those choices and why they fit your student, and as much – or as little – help with the process as you need. You also get an objective third party to help push the application process and encourage your student to get things done on a reasonable time table. This leaves time for you as a parent to be a cheerleader rather than constant nag about what has been done or not. As a parent, this in itself can be worth a lot!

Now, let's talk about costs. A good consultant will charge anywhere between $80 to well over $100 per hour for their time. Their services are not cheap, but as the cliché goes, you get what you pay for. If you choose your mechanic, financial advisor, and attorney based on cost alone, you will probably get lousy advice. Choose a private counselor who spends a great deal of time and money in traveling to colleges, attending conferences, and meeting admission reps, and you will probably find it money well spent. Also, put things in perspective. Calling an electrician or plumber will probably cost more per hour than the work of a professional counselor.

Which brings us to a good question: Is any of this fair? Why should families even consider paying for advice they can get for free at their high school? The answer is because most high schools invest more time and money on their football and basketball teams than quality college counseling. It is because admission to places like Harvard and Stanford are in the single digits. Also, because it is ultimately an investment – not a cost – that will serve Johnny or Mary well long after their senior year.

Choosing the Best
College for You

Rankings: If It Is a "Known and Highly-Ranked" School, Then It Must Be Good . . . Right?

> ## Take-away:
> *Rankings are useful but not the be-all and end-all, so be careful!*

Perception is reality. The problem is that the value of the rankings only takes you so far in the college selection process. College rankings are a quick and easy way to sift through the thousands of choices out there. If anything else, it gives you a broad list of options that you may not have thought of or did not even know existed. It's a good starting point because it categorizes the choices into different tiers and gives you a ton of statistics about colleges all in one place.

However, beyond this initial filtering, understand the limitations on rankings. As with any institution, colleges and universities are marketing themselves and working toward doing what they need to get a higher ranking. This is hardly surprising; colleges are businesses that can – and sometimes do – go bankrupt if they don't attract enough students. Not to mention the fact that when you are getting down into the details, the rankings are ultimately based on subjective judgment.

Here are some reasons why you need to be careful about getting too caught up in the rankings when it's time to search for the college that is right for your student. First, the rankings cluster colleges/ universities into larger buckets, such as *most selective, more selective,* and *selective,* that seem to be helpful. But when it comes down to the details of College X being ranked #25 and College Y stands at #24, you really can't distinguish them for all practical purposes – so don't try. The value of the ranking in college selection ends when it is on that level. That's when you have to jump in and figure out what matters to your teen and what the best fit is for them. Don't let someone else do it for you.

Just because a school rejects a lot of students does not necessarily mean that it is a better school. Just because an institution has famous Nobel Prize-winning professors does not mean you will ever see them or take a class from them.

Rankings can make education a bit cookie cutter in terms of what is considered the right way of educating kids. Rankings do not humanize the experience and can turn into a bit of a numbers game comprised of test scores, percentiles, and other stats. The social and educational experience of the student is ultimately what matters. Rankings can turn into a self-fulfilling prophecy where the same schools are known and ranked high and therefore continue to be ranked high because everyone knows about them and also expects them to be good.

So explore more deeply using your unique criteria once you have narrowed the search to a small set of schools. When it comes down to it, what type of educational and social atmosphere will make your student feel comfortable while also challenged? Ask yourself how the departments and professors are viewed in the majors that your child is interested in. Are there any special programs or approaches to educating that best fit your child, such as freshmen experiences or programs where like-minded students live in the same dorms? What are the options for study abroad programs, internships, and research experiences? How accessible are professors for mentoring and advising? Are there opportunities to work with professors one-on-one? What are the statistics on graduates in terms of job and graduate school placement, particularly in the fields of study that your student is interested in?

Rankings can start you on the journey, but don't get caught into the trap of "keeping up with the Joneses" and getting mesmerized in the bright lights of certain schools that everyone holds in awe. There are many options out there, so use the rankings wisely as a way to identify a wide variety of potential schools. Then, focus on what matters to your student and family. The ultimate question is: Which school will be the best fit and provide the educational opportunities that will challenge your teen to achieve his or her goals?

The Well-Known Schools
Are The Only Ones That Matter
-- Fact or Fiction?

The Well-Known Schools are the Only Ones That Matter – Fact or Fiction?

> Take-away:
> *Who cares if people know about a school?*

We know that many people would disagree with this opinion, but we feel strongly that the majority of Americans know about any particular college or university because . . . the school has a really, really good sports team.

Think we're kidding?

Ask a random sampling of ten people to name four or five "good" colleges around the country (more on what a "good" college looks like later). Likely, the first choice will be the local branch of State U. Following close behind may be one of the Ivy League schools such as Harvard or Yale. After that, you'll likely hear names like Penn State, Miami, Ohio State, or the University of North Carolina. Apart from the Ivy League schools, the only thing that these institutions really have in common is that they play in big time sports conferences that attract tens of thousands of fans to every football, basketball, or baseball game. They also happen to be on ESPN constantly from September through May.

Word of mouth can often be good, but not when it comes to picking your college. It is human nature to make strong associations to things you hear about all the time from friends and family. If Aunt Barbara or your buddy Bill thinks that the local college is the best thing since apple pie, and you hear that constantly, it will affect your impressions of that school. Yet our friends, family, coworkers – they have all been exposed to the same informational resources that lead us to know about a given school based on all the wrong criteria.

The stunning reality that often surprises families is that some of the *least* known colleges carry the greatest weight in academic prestige, career preparation, and graduate school admission statistics. For example, take Oberlin College in Ohio. We would be willing to bet that you've never heard of the school, which is understandable. It has no Division I sports teams, it is located near much-maligned Cleveland, and it is a small school. Yet you may be surprised to know that Oberlin was the first school in America to regularly admit African-Americans and women and boasts one of the best liberal arts programs in the country. In fact, it has been one of the best for quite some time.

What you may also not know is that Oberlin carries tremendous weight with graduate school admissions departments from around the country because of the quality of the academic curriculum. Even though Oberlin is a relatively small school, it has a surprisingly good track record in providing financial aid for needy students.

Not bad for a school that most of the population has never heard of!

The unfortunate reality is that when colleges visit high schools every fall, seniors usually only want to hear representatives from schools that they know about. The local state university will have large numbers of attendees at their seminar. School such as Oberlin may have one or two students who show up to listen.

Our advice? Look for the diamond in the rough, ignore the so-called "name" schools that friends and family embrace, and make good decisions that are in your best interest. Spend the time looking at schools near and far with a focus on what really matters, and you may be very surprised to find out that very high quality schools have zero name recognition with your friends. With so many great schools around the country, you deserve to be a choosy consumer.

What Role Does Political and Social Orientation Play in College Choices?

Take-away:
Don't limit yourself because of politics; open your mind and really look at the choice with the end in mind.

There is a lot of media attention about our current political polarization. The country seems to be split right down the middle. Cable television shows seem to feed us all what we want to hear, whatever our political and social views are on any issue. Often there are angry discussions about how our educational system is biased and about how political correctness influences what students learn and value.

With this backdrop comes the challenge for parents to determine what type of environment is best suited for their teens. It comes down to our comfort level with ourselves as parents and the degree of trust we have in our kids. It also requires a vision of what type of college experience we want our kids to have and what we envision for them in the future.

For us, it comes down to a few questions that you have to ask yourselves as parents:

1. Does looking for a college that matches your political beliefs necessarily mean a good educational experience for

your kid – whether it is liberal or conservative or any other political persuasion for that matter?

2. Do you trust your kid to be able to sort out what he or she believes so that they can embrace and create their own points of view?

3. Are you able to let go and look for what is best for your kid's short and long-term goals and find the best fit for them where they will flourish and are situated for future success?

Nelson and his family went through this journey as they sorted through the options and asked themselves as a family the questions above. In fact, after they asked themselves these questions, they broadened the search and added colleges not on the original list.

Ultimately, what you will find is that top-notch colleges cannot be easily characterized. These colleges have a wide range of groups on campus with a diverse set of beliefs. Of course, there is often a predominant political and/or social vibe that should be considered. For example, for the most part Berkeley will always be liberal and Oral Roberts University will always be conservative. But the fact is that college environments are a microcosm of the world at large and can be an enriching and safe place to learn about other perspectives and also to develop and defend one's views. The decision of what is acceptable or not for a student and family is theirs alone, but we strongly recommend that you don't too quickly dismiss institutions because of what you have heard and/or read in the guidebooks. Stereotypes can be dangerous concerning colleges as well as people.

When it comes to education, being with people that all believe what you do may not be the best educational environment . Sometimes some constructive debate and conflict can sharpen the mind and also solidify a student's personal views. No matter what, don't limit your options because of political and social orientation because you may be limiting the long-term growth of your teen and actually doing the very thing that you are trying to avoid.

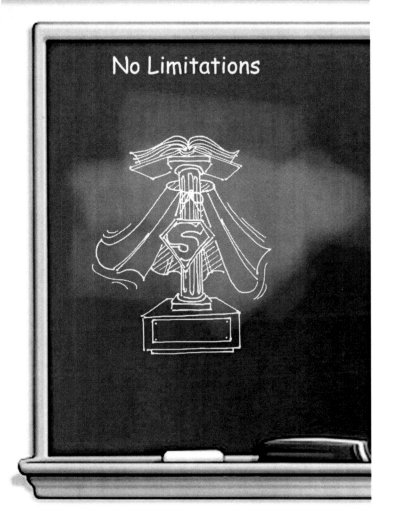

No Limitations

Take-away:

Shoot for the stars as long as you can, then pare the list down when you have to.

There is a tendency for families to think of all the reasons why a particular college is out of reach or won't work for their kid. Here are the more common reasons:

- It's too expensive
- It's too far/close from home
- It's too big/small
- It's in the middle of nowhere/too urban
- It's too liberal/conservative

The point is that it is very easy to create barriers right off the bat because of our insecurities, fears, and concerns.

But start off with an open mind! There will be time for taking colleges off the list. Start by thinking really big. Come up with a "wish list" of dream schools where you can imagine yourself and visualize what it would be like.

The college search will have its twists and turns, but we truly believe that the journey should begin as wide and as broad as possible. Rather than identifying factors that immediately limit choices, we believe you should use these same factors as ways of expanding the search.

Why be broad? Starting without limitations can broaden your family's thinking about what options are possible. Starting out without limitations can energize students to dream and really push them to think about what they want out of college. Starting without limitations can open up communication between parents and kids by encouraging discussions about what they like and dislike. All of these outcomes mean kids may take more ownership of the process. It will likely also open a pathway to family conversation. This also has benefits for parents because this time of transition is not easy on parents either. It's an emotional time for mom and dad as they deal with letting go of their kids to the college scene.

The major benefit of creating the "wish list" of dream schools is it gets the mental juices flowing about the criteria for selecting the list of colleges. It also identifies barriers that need to be addressed. It could be objective factors such as test scores and letters of recommendations that need a stronger focus. It could also be fears, concerns, and misunderstandings that need to be addressed.

This exercise gets families to identify the issues and develop a set of criteria that will form the foundation for the family strategy. What matters to parents and kids? What are the hot buttons to watch out for? How do we identify the specific criteria that will help us pick the right school? What additional information do we need to help us decide?

Shoot for the moon. Expand rather than contract. Go for it!

Don't Let The Price Tag Fool You

Don't Let the Price Tag Fool You

Take-away:
Look beyond the sticker price; focus on the fit. It may not be as expensive as you think.

Selecting a college is like saving for retirement. It is deciding to invest and give up something today for the long-term benefit it provides tomorrow. Okay, it is a little different than retirement because these days the cost of college for your kid seems like investing *a lot* today for potential, uncertain benefits tomorrow. Going to Harvard, Princeton, Yale, or Stanford is a pipe dream unless my family makes a gazillion dollars, right?

Think again.

Don't limit your search or your dreams too soon. Never let money be the initial obstacle. Like buying a car, don't be fooled by the sticker price. After all, you don't care about the price the car manufacturer wants, you only care about what you want to pay. Similarly, the actual out-of-pocket costs of a major college or university are usually far less than what they advertise. Rarely do families pay full price.

You won't know if it is possible unless you try. Put yourself in the game by doing the work. Figure out if you meet the basic academic requirements, and if you do, give it a try. Fill out the FAFSA.

Research the schools that interest you regardless of "sticker price." For example, there are colleges and universities such as Harvard, MIT, Stanford, and University of California schools (think Berkeley and UCLA) that are committed to reducing student educational debt by limiting student loans in financial aid packages. Websites such as www.ProjectOnStudentDebt.org are there to help as well.

If you have done the hard work and have achieved academically then you should have multiple college options available to you. With literally thousands of four-year colleges out there, the odds are heavily in *your* favor. Keep your dreams alive as long as you can. Don't start from a position of limitation and constraint based on finances. If you don't try, you won't know if it is possible.

Families often look at the price tag of a college and decide a school is too expensive. Once school costs are driving the process, the tendency is for the student to apply only to those schools with the lowest tuition costs. Costs, rather than educational excellence, wind up driving the process.

Once you prioritize costs over all else, you lose sight of the big picture. A college's bank account, or endowment, tells you how much money it has available for student financial aid. The less money a school has in its endowment, the less money it can offer your son or daughter. It is a simple matter of economics.

When you look at where to apply, focus first on the standards, reputation, and ranking of the colleges. Then look at the size of the school's endowment. Typing "endowment" and "college" into Google pulls up this list quickly. You will be pleased to know that most of the nation's "prestige" colleges also have the most money available for financial aid. This is important because they are expensive schools, so the financial aid makes them accessible to almost all Americans.

As crazy as it may seem, many parents pay more for low-cost public colleges than they would have for expensive private colleges. Although public colleges charge less, they have smaller endowment funds. So Johnny might get into State U. with a "reasonable" $10,000 per year tuition, but mom and dad will often be responsible for most of that burden. Contrast that with Harvard, which guarantees that all admitted students with family incomes at a middle-class level will receive 100% non-repayable financial aid. In other words, a full ride. This does not even tap scholarships that might recognize your teen's special skills and achievements. For example, in some schools, if you can play the bagpipe you might find yourself getting a scholarship.

Don't put the cart before the horse. Choose colleges based on academic excellence and what excites Johnny and Mary. You wouldn't choose a car based purely on the price tag because you value reliability, safety, and performance. Don't make the college search the equivalent of hunting in the bargain bin at the local discount outlet.

Be A Selective Consumer

Be a Selective Consumer

> Take-away:
> *The majority of colleges are competing for your teen's matriculation and money.*

The popular media would have you believe that plenty of schools around the country are as hard to get into as Harvard, Stanford, and Yale. We call such schools "Über U" because they are so intensely competitive that in a *good* year one out of every ten applicants will receive an offer of admission.

Understandably, many high-achieving high school seniors are worried that they won't get into their top choices. In fact, some students worry they won't get in anywhere – a paranoia driven by the media telling kids how tough it's going to be to get into a great school.

The opposite is true. Most colleges are paranoid that your kid won't be applying to their school!

Let's shoot down one myth about admission rates. Harvard and Yale's admission rates are nowhere near representative of the vast majority of schools in the country. Most colleges accept most of their applicants. Unless you are driven by a kamikaze mentality and only apply to Ivy League-type schools, you will get in *somewhere* that fits your needs and interests. Ironically, many of America's best colleges are the ones competing for your kid.

Why are small liberal arts colleges the most likely to be competing for your kid's matriculation and money? Because they suffer from a perception problem. Families think they are too expensive, and when families are cutting costs many won't even consider a private liberal arts education. We've heard of many families during tough economic times say that they don't want their teens to major in something that won't land them a job after graduation. Unfortunately, small liberal arts colleges often get unfairly blamed for not providing students with marketable skills for the job market. (By the way, this idea is absurd – these colleges wouldn't have thrived for hundreds of years if they did a miserable job of preparing students for jobs.)

Let's address the cost issue. Liberal arts colleges generally do have ample resources for financial aid, precisely because they come with such high price tags. We can tell you who is *not* competing for your son or daughter to attend: State U. A large state university knows they can reliably expect a large applicant pool year in and year out. Those numbers skyrocket during tough economic times because more families think – often incorrectly – that State U. will be the cheaper option. So from the state university's perspective, there is no incentive whatsoever to compete for your son or daughter. Come if you'd like, but if not, someone else will take your seat.

But the smaller schools, and especially the private ones, can and will aggressively market their liberal arts programs to high school students. If your kid is applying to multiple small private liberal arts colleges – which we recommend – chances are high that those schools will go the extra mile to put together a financial aid package that will be extremely attractive to your family.

We recommend that you look at the college admission process from a totally new perspective. Rather than seeing your kid trying hard to get through the door of their dream college, you should see the colleges and universities as competing ferociously to get your kid through their front door. Therefore, be a selective consumer. Ask probing questions. Really look at the academic and social environment and identify programs and student organizations that ignite your kid's passions and interests. Be assertive in asking about financial aid options. Learn if the school offers merit-based financial aid. Quiz school officials about their track record of getting their graduates into top law schools, medical schools, and doctoral programs.

You are in the driver's seat. You are about to commit yourself to one of the largest financial expenditures in your lifetime. To the thousands of colleges and universities across the United States, your teen is a precious asset, and you should leverage your unique capacity – especially if you are applying to college during tough economic times.

Long-Term View

Take-away:

Few motivated students will stop at a bachelor's degree; always be thinking of what colleges will open doors to top graduate schools.

At the time of this writing, the Great Recession that began in 2007 is still in full force. The United States is suffering from almost 10% unemployment, millions of people have difficulty even getting a job interview, and countless more have completely stopped searching for work. In fact, policymakers say that many of the jobs lost during the Great Recession may never come back.

While this may be a bleak outlook, it does illustrate one important fact of working in the modern age. You're no longer competing simply against bright people in your city or state – you are competing against the world. American college grads now have to battle for jobs with people overseas who would gladly do their work for much lower wages. And technology now allows employers to outsource virtually any kind of work to lower-paid, highly-skilled employees in any corner of the world. In fact, in these times, one of the best sources of job security and the highest ROI (return on investment) is to have a college education from a top-notch institution. According to a PayScale wage study, the average thirty year net return on investment for 554 colleges/ universities is 9%, and MIT had a thirty year net return on investment of nearly $1.7 million (http://www.payscale.com/2008-best-colleges).

What does this have to do with college admissions?

It means that we are no longer living in a manufacturing economy; we now operate in a knowledge-based economy. People who will remain highly compensated in relatively secure jobs are going to be young people who obtain a world-class education that provides them with the tools to be indispensable workers. It also means that students must gain credentials that demonstrate their knowledge to employers; this is of paramount importance. Not all students, even before the Great Recession, went immediately into the workforce after receiving a bachelor's degree. We would argue that not only is that pattern going to continue, but that in many ways a bachelor's degree is only marginally better than what a high school degree was a generation ago.

We think that there should be a complete rethinking of what college is all about. For the vast majority of students and families reading this book, college will not be the last formal education a student receives. Far from it. Many students who seek to obtain the skills to remain indispensable to organizations will go on to graduate school – be it a law degree, master's or Ph.D., or medical degree. We urge you to no longer look at college as a way to obtain skills for the job market, although that is important, but rather as a stepping stone to graduate school. If you follow our logic that highly-skilled employees will invariably have advanced degrees, then it make sense to evaluate colleges based upon their track record of getting their students into top-flight graduate schools.

But how do you do that? As we've mentioned in earlier chapters, colleges and universities see students as their most valuable asset, particularly small private colleges. If you are about to embark upon the second most important financial commitment you ever make, next to your house, then you deserve good and precise answers to the following questions: What percentage of your graduates go on to graduate school? Specifically, what universities do your graduates attend, especially concerning law, medicine, and Ph.D. programs? You may wish to visit the admissions office of a highly-regarded law or medical school in your area and ask those officials which colleges seem to be producing top-flight students for their program.

Scour the Internet for this information as well. Many graduate schools publicize the colleges that send students to their institution. You're likely to see the same schools pop up again and again, not only because those colleges attract great students but also because they prepare students for the rigors and demands of graduate school in a way that sets them apart from their peers.

The most important thing to remember in the college search is to ensure that when your son or daughter receives their degree, that they also have obtained a passport to a top-flight graduate program of their choosing. Your college should implicitly promise that if your son or daughter does well at their institution that they will go on to a good graduate program. If they can't or won't, then you are making a very poor investment and you are likely not providing your son or daughter with the credentialing skills required to compete for choice graduate school slots – or for the global economy. Also consider the fact that if your kid has been prepared for the rigors of future education, they also have been prepared for life!

Criteria for Selection

Safety

Take-away:
Most colleges, even in urban areas, are completely safe.

Here's a trivia question: What does the Johns Hopkins University, the University of Pennsylvania, and the University of Chicago all have in common – besides the fact that they are terrific universities?

They happen to be situated in relatively unattractive urban areas. Baltimore, Philadelphia, and the South Side of Chicago are not reassuring places for many families about to send their kids off to college.

Many parents understandably want to ensure that when their students go away to college that they're living in absolute safety. This is part of the reason why families love to take their kids to visit colleges and universities during the junior and senior year. They go on campus tours and try to get a feel for the campus during the several hours they spend there. By the way, rarely do they spend more than a few hours on any given tour because they often over-schedule campus visits. In fact, the only interaction a family might experience at a college is with a student tour guide – who is typically paid by the college.

Because these campus visits are so short in duration, many families try to pick up on clues as to the safety of an institution given its surroundings. However, we believe based upon many intensive visits to schools across the country that there is no college or university in the United States that we would automatically disqualify purely based upon safety. In fact, despite the fact that Hopkins, U. Penn, and Chicago are all situated in blighted urban areas, they still retain sky-high prestige not only among graduate schools but also among employers and prospective students.

The reality of public safety at virtually all colleges and universities in the United States is that they are perfectly safe so long as students use common sense. First, students who go to school in an urban area go through an orientation where they are made aware of basic safety precautions to take. Second, colleges go the extra mile to ensure that students have all the relevant information they need regarding campus safety so they can adjust their behavior accordingly. Paradoxically, the students who go to colleges in small towns or in so-called low crime areas often let their guard down and may be more at risk for property crimes just because of the perceived lack of danger in the area.

Most importantly, keep in mind that there is a perfect overlap of incentives between families and the colleges when it comes to safety. A college knows that it depends upon its reputation and needs incoming students each year to allow the institution to survive. If a college does not take every reasonable step to ensure the safety of its student body, the college will simply go out of business. That's precisely why schools like the University of Chicago and the University of Southern California, both located in urban areas, have remarkably low rates of violent crime. Even their property crime rates are not dramatically different than they are at other large schools in less urban areas. Schools accept a moral, legal, and, yes, financial obligation to ensure that their students, staff, and faculty are living and working in a safe environment.

Finally, consider that students who are living in dormitories rarely leave campus to go into large urban areas. Whether it's visiting with friends, attending fraternity and sorority parties, or simply studying, college students have all the facilities and resources they need on campus. The dorms will be the epicenter of their social life, and the few times that a student goes into a downtown urban area are often when friends and family come to visit or when the university or college itself sponsors an event off campus. It is fairly rare for students to depend heavily upon activities in the city as opposed to enjoying all the social benefits offered by a college or university right on campus.

We're parents too, so we completely understand why safety is always a consideration. It would be nice to assign a personal bodyguard to each of our children – especially when they first leave home. However, there is no need to worry about the public safety situation at the schools your teen is considering. Based on our campus visits and our experiences with students, colleges do an exceptional job of ensuring that students are living and working in a thriving, safe, and collaborative environment.

Sports

Sports

Take-away:
There is an almost perfect inverse relationship between sports emphasis and quality academics.

The Ivy League didn't establish its elite credentials on the football field. Just ask Columbia University about their football team. Between 1983 and 1988, the Columbia Lions lost 44 consecutive games. Their team was so unlucky on the field that the marching band literally resorted to playing the "Mickey Mouse Club" song in mocking salute to the gridiron team. Other teams that have racked up impressive losing streaks in recent years include Northwestern, Oberlin, Caltech and even Duke (the football team, not the basketball team).

One of the reasons we laugh about losing streaks such as Columbia's is because it strikes us as funny that a school so renowned for academics could be so woeful on the field (in football, anyway). In fact, there seems to be an almost direct correlation between high-quality colleges and universities and mediocre athletic performance. While there are some spectacular exceptions, such as the University of Michigan, Stanford, and the University of Texas, the simple truth is that many prestigious colleges and universities in the United States do *not* have a strong reputation for athletics and do not place a great emphasis on how they perform in sports.

On the other hand, consider some of the schools that are famous for the quality of their sports. You may wish to Google whether those schools have been sanctioned by the NCAA (the governing body for college sports) for improper behavior. In fact, some of the most cherished names in college athletics have been sanctioned for conduct unbecoming an institution of higher education. Some universities have been accused of tolerating athletes on campus who have engaged in criminal behavior. Academic administrators at some well-known schools have often looked the other way while the athletic department essentially ran a separate kingdom within these institutions. It's unfortunate, but it will likely come as no surprise to many parents that big time sports at some of America's colleges and universities have supplanted academic excellence as an institutional priority.

If a student is using the quality of the sports teams as the criterion for choosing a college, we think that the student is making a serious mistake. Without sounding preachy, we don't think families should be forking over potentially $50,000 or more a year so that a kid can watch a football game or a basketball game in a packed stadium or arena. You're in school to obtain a world-class education necessary to compete in the global economy. In fact, the students that are prioritizing sports over such considerations as class size, academic reputation, and financial resources need to take a step back and reorganize the college search around more important long-term priorities.

We also need to move away from the idea that only Division I schools (schools offering sports scholarships) offer a terrific sports environment on college campuses. Division II or Division III schools, which do not offer athletic scholarships, also offer rewarding sports experiences both for athletes and for spectators. For example, Washington University in St. Louis, a Division III school, does not award scholarships for women's volleyball. Yet, the school has developed an impressive reputation for winning Division III titles in women's volleyball, and attending one of these games at Wash U's Field House is an experience not to be missed.

We believe strongly, as we suspect you do, that we have elevated sports too much in this country and that we have lost perspective on the role it should play not only in academia but also in society. For students who are seeking to watch entertaining sports events or to participate at a high level of competition, we would urge them to take a look at Division II and Division III schools which may offer them a terrific competitive experience. We would also recommend that families never lose a laser-like focus on the reasons for attending school. With the reality that virtually any job can be outsourced to Bangalore or Shanghai, and with increasing competition for choice slots at graduate schools, why would any family see sports as a major criterion in the college search?

One last note: We sometimes meet students who play sports in high school for the sole reason of trying to win a scholarship for college. We think this is a poor strategy for the vast majority of teens because most students are not going to win a full ride to college based upon their athletic skills. Millions of American high schoolers play organized sports, and the odds are that you're unlikely to win that coveted athletic scholarship. Even if you do win the scholarship, the college is not giving it to you cost-free; you will be expected to practice continuously throughout your education, which may negatively impact your studies and may cloud your priorities about why you are attending college in the first place.

Make a wise choice and place sports in its proper context during the college admissions process.

It's a College, Not a Resort

Take-away:
"Look at that athletic facility – the college must be good."
Think again; the primary reason for going to college is the
education!

Colleges are carrying out a marketing full-court press to attract your teen. The result is an arms race between institutions to do whatever it takes to attract the attention of the best students. In fact, college marketing campaigns rival anything that global behemoths McDonald's, Coca-Cola, or Ford produces. And why not? Colleges have the right to put their institution in the best possible light. They are running a business that needs to continue to attract and retain customers, namely your kids, with the blessing and financial support of you as parents.

So, families need to keep their eyes on the prize when it comes to the college search. Ultimately, the primary goal is to find the best academic fit and overall environment for the student.

What parents will see in terms of marketing to their kids and the facilities and amenities on campuses will not resemble what we experienced a generation ago. Beware of the glitz and don't get distracted by it. Remember, your kid is selecting a college, not a resort or vacation destination. Some of the areas to look at with interest and a bit of healthy skepticism are marketing material, campus tours, award-winning professors, and sports facilities.

Once your kid takes a pre-standardized test (PLAN, PSAT), they will be inundated with impressive, glossy materials telling the student about the unbelievable virtues and assets of many colleges. They will also begin to get personal letters and even phone calls from the colleges. This personal contact can make a student feel very special and wanted. Not a bad thing, of course, but it may unduly increase their interest in a college even if it is not a good fit. Only your family, and ultimately, your high schooler can discover a college that matches a student's interests, background, and aspirations.

Campus tours aren't just a boring walking tour around the campus with a current college student anymore. In fact, some campus tours include bikes, boats, buses, golf carts, and even GPS devices and iPhone apps to create unique campus visits. Again, the goal is to create a memorable experience for students and families while they are visiting the college and to give them a sense of what it is like. Real life on campus will not include a boat or a GPS device to take you around campus. It comes down to whether the college is a good fit.

Colleges will also do a lot to attract nationally-renowned professors, including recruiting them with six-figure salaries and generous benefits. Colleges want to say in their brochures that they have X% of Ph.D.'s and Nobel Prize winners, and landed the professor that discovered or cured Y. As consumers, college-bound families need to step back out of the glow of the statistics and ask themselves some questions: How often do these professors ever teach undergraduates? What is the likelihood that the student will ever take a class from these famous professors? Are these professors in fields that are of interest to the student?

Facilities are bigger, better, and often architectural wonders. Gone are the days of dingy dorms, tasteless cafeteria food, and bare bones extras. Touring a college campus today reveals Olympic-caliber gyms and swimming pools, gourmet cafeterias, posh dormitories, skating rinks, art and film centers, hot tubs, and state-of-the-art technology. In fact, some campuses have horse stables and luxury condo-like apartments. Is this a college campus or a luxury resort? Again, these amenities are wonderful to have and understandably excite high school students. But parents and students have to ask themselves, is the college experience about paying for gourmet meals and luxury recreation?

Knowing that colleges are "selling" to you, it is your family's responsibility to look beyond the splashy marketing and the glitzy amenities to find the right college. Don't get enamored and distracted with all the bright lights and glitz. What matters is that the place really fits your kid's interests, learning style, and academic competitiveness. At the same time, your college choices must provide the right kind of physical and social environment for them to have an overall enriching college experience. Decide what the non-negotiable items are and keep your eye on the real prize.

Frats And Sororities

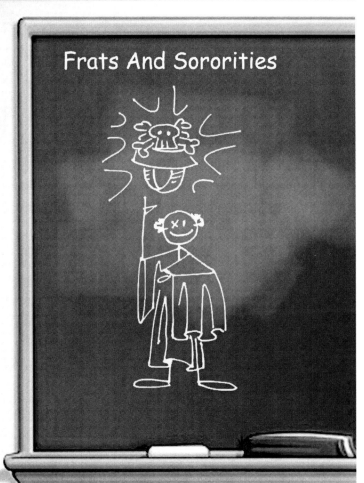

Frats and Sororities

Take-away:
Frats and Sororities can be an enriching experience, but think of time, money, and focus before pledging and jumping into that scene.

National Lampoon's 1978 film classic *Animal House* chronicles the adventures of two freshmen pledges Larry Kroger (Pinto) and Kent Dorfman (Flounder) and their fraternity brothers at Delta Tau Chi. Remember the great scenes with John Belushi's character John "Bluto" Blutarsky?

Clearly, the escapades chronicled in movies such as *Animal House* are an exaggerated picture of what goes on in fraternities and sororities, right?

Or are they accurate?

In the spirit of full disclosure, Jason and Nelson were not members of a fraternity. However, we admit to visiting frats and sororities on a few weekends during our college career as a social excursion and educational experience (not for the free beer, of course). So, although we have many friends who jointed frats and sororities, our view will be an outsider's view of the whole experience. From our viewpoint, kids and parents have to balance the pros and cons of attending an institution that has frats and sororities on campus and, if they do, the decision to join one.

Some of the positives that can come out of fraternity or sorority membership revolve around the social and personal growth opportunities that come from quickly joining an existing group and organizational structure. It's a sense of belonging and a pre-existing, ready-made social group that the student gets to plug into. Many of these groups have a community service and philanthropic culture that can be personally enriching. Through the organization there are leadership opportunities that can help the student grow and develop. It can also be a good source of mentoring and support for the student in a close-knit community. Finally, these organizations potentially provide the student a short- and long-term network that can be used for graduate school and job opportunities during and after college.

These positives have to be balanced against the potential downsides. Some believe that fraternities and sororities are too exclusive and create a bad social scene for everyone. There is some truth to the often-repeated taunt that you are "paying for friends" when you pledge a frat or sorority. Furthermore, these organizations can create group behavior that is unhealthy, from binge drinking to hazing. In some cases, the social scene and hanging out with your fellow members takes precedence over education. Think of kids sleeping late into the day with remnants of the previous night all around them. Membership can also cost a lot, so financial considerations need to be factored in. There is also the potential time drain on social and/or community service activities.

Only you know your teen and his or her ability to put fraternity and sorority membership in its proper place. Any good thing can turn bad quickly if not properly managed. Will the club mentality mean that your student will go with the crowd and participate in unhealthy activities to the extreme? Will all the social activities mean that school work takes a back seat? Does the close-knit community of the frat or sorority mean that your kid will not interact with other students?

We can't decide for you, but we feel strongly that social organizations and activities should be kept in their proper place. Ultimately, it is a judgment call by the individual. However, really think hard about why you are sending your kid to college and whether the pros outweigh the cons for each individual based on their personality. Focus on what college is about. Determine how much money and time should be invested in these activities over other potential experiences. We made our decision about frats decades ago. Now it is your teen's turn.

"Cool City"

Take-away:
Most students' social life is in the dorm environment.

San Francisco, Boston, and New York City are among the most attractive destinations for tourists. They offer glimmering lights, gourmet restaurants, and arts and entertainment. Millions of tourists visit these cities each year because they are America's world-class metropolises. Unsurprisingly, the enthusiasm tourists have in visiting these cities also translates into thousands of American high school students wanting to attend college in the City by the Bay, Beantown, and the Big Apple.

However, it is much different being a tourist in these cities than being a college student. It's terrific if the college search ends up leading your kid to one of these fabulous cities. But our strong advice is to not put too much emphasis on the location of your colleges and universities.

The reason? For most students it really doesn't matter *where* their school is located.

Take for example such elite schools as Yale, Dartmouth, Cornell, and Brown. These schools are located, respectively, in New Haven, Connecticut; Hanover, New Hampshire; Ithaca, New York; and

Providence, Rhode Island. None of these locales are on the radar screen for most tourists. In the case of New Haven, many would find the town to be rather bleak (but with outstanding pizza!). But who cares?

The fact is that a student who is attending college is going to spend most of his or her time on campus, not only for studying but also for recreation. Students will quickly find that their dormitories are the epicenter of their social life, whether it be playing card games, attending an after-exam party, or simply hanging out with friends. Students who live in a dorm usually don't have a car, so a lack of mobility inevitably leads them to make the most out of living on campus. Students are generally not hanging out at Fisherman's Wharf, Faneuil Hall, or Times Square, but rather are building important and long-lasting friendships with their peers in the residence halls.

Another common argument that we hear is that it's important to live in an exciting city because of the internship and externships available. The thinking goes like this: if you're going to school in, say, Washington DC, then you have a much better chance of securing an internship with a federal agency. This is complete nonsense. Almost every major university in the United States can easily set up an internship opportunity in Washington and other major cities. In fact, many colleges even have satellite campuses or university-owned apartments in cities like Washington that allow their students to temporarily live in those cities while doing their internships. In an interconnected world, we are increasingly seeing colleges broadening the scope of what their students can do and where they can do it.

Our advice to parents is to make location a secondary consideration in the college search. Just because your kid goes to college in Boston or San Francisco does not mean they are getting any better of an education than someone going to school in a rural area or a midsize city. Our strongly-held belief is that college ultimately is a pathway to getting a high-quality education and ultimately into a good graduate school and secure employment. We have seen no evidence whatsoever that attending school in a glamorous American city gives you any advantage in succeeding in graduate school admissions or professional advancement.

We love San Francisco, Boston, and New York. However, you should keep in mind the difference between being a visitor and a four-year resident at a college.

Graduate School

Take-away:
Look beyond today and start with the end in mind. How will graduate schools and future employers look at your college of choice?

It may seem crazy to be wondering about graduate school and/or future employment potential given all that your family is going through at this very moment. But guess what? It is not crazy and in fact very wise to be looking to the future!

If you think of education and the selection of a college as an investment, then due diligence and a long-term view make total sense. It's like Warren Buffett's value investment strategy. Buffett states, "Only buy something that you'd be perfectly happy to hold if the market shut down for ten years," adding, "Value is what you get." The college selection process is very similar to Buffett's view of investment. Is the college a place worth investing in for the long haul, and will its value increase over time?

College costs have soared, so many families are debating the value their kids will get out of the investment. Short-term costs can be intimidating and downright scary. So the future value that your kids will get because of the investment is a serious factor in deciding what to do and therefore needs to be part of the equation. Spend time thinking about the future because it matters! In fact, federal data indicate that the more education a person has, the lower unemployment and higher wages they will experience. According to a U.S. Census Bureau report entitled "The Big Payoff: Educational attainment and synthetic estimates of work-life earnings," the more education a person has, the more money they will make in their lifetime. The numbers are staggering; high school graduates can expect $1.2 million in lifetime earnings; bachelor's degree holders $2.1 million; master's degree recipients $2.5 million; doctoral degree graduates $3.4 million; and professional degree holders $4.4 million.

As you look at colleges, ask yourself some key questions not unlike what Buffett has said about investing.

Consider:

- What percentage of graduates received job offers after graduation and what were the types of jobs and starting salaries?
- What percentage of students got accepted to graduate schools in their chosen field of study and what fields were they?
- What are graduates doing in their careers? This is related to the potential alumni network that students can tap into and also the reputation the institution has in the workplace.
- Where did faculty members get their degrees and what are they currently doing in their fields?
- How recognized are the faculty in their fields? This gets at the type of recommendations students receive and how well-regarded the institution is in the general academic community.

- What type of reputation does the institution have in the local community, nationally, and internationally? Is it recognized in publications, rankings, and the general community?

Look to the long-term benefits. Don't be short-sighted. What's the buzz about the institution in the world at large? The broader and wider the buzz, the greater the long-term value of the investment. There are many schools with similar short-term costs; look to the long-term to differentiate between them.

Rankings

Take-away:
They do matter.

There is a famous joke about workers in the old Soviet Union:

"We pretend to work; they pretend to pay us."

Part of the reason why we love this joke is because it illustrates the hypocrisy that went on between Soviet workers and the communist government. Without taking the analogy too far, we feel that the way that colleges treat rankings – especially the U.S. News & World Report rankings – is just like this old Soviet joke. The colleges pretend not to care what the rankings say, and the parents pretend that they care about what the colleges are saying about the rankings.

Let's be clear about this. We love college rankings. They educate parents and keep the colleges accountable for their educational product. But you wouldn't know it from the colleges. In fact, it is exceedingly rare for a college or university – especially a prestigious one – to go on the record to say that U.S. News & World Report's rankings bear any resemblance to reality. It is often striking how colleges go the extra mile to de-emphasize and de-legitimize school rankings. However, we believe strongly that rankings such as U.S. News & World Report's do have a major role to play in how you select what colleges and universities your kid applies to. There are many reasons for this.

First, don't believe the colleges when they say that they don't care about rankings. Perhaps the colleges that are downplaying the rankings are those that don't do well in them. Sour grapes? They really do care. They invest enormous amounts of time and money to improve in areas that hurt them in the rankings. Some of these criteria may include their admission rate, average SAT and GPA of incoming freshmen, or the percentage of alumni who contribute to the school. They know precisely what the criteria are for the rankings, and they do address weak spots behind the scenes. Colleges are, at their core, businesses. They have to balance their books, make payroll, and make sure they have a new crop of students each year. They also know that millions of American families read these rankings and take their cues from those rankings. For colleges not to try to improve their rankings given the importance they play in the college search would be financial recklessness.

There's another important reason why rankings matter; they do reflect, to a certain degree, the reality of how colleges are perceived not only by graduate schools but also by employers. What is remarkable is that of the top twenty-five schools in the U.S. News & World Report rankings, there have not been dramatic changes on a year-to-year basis. In fact, our experience has been that the top twenty-five schools in the U.S. News & World Report rankings mirror the most respected undergraduate programs as perceived by graduate school admissions officers. The reason is that the rankings take into account legitimate criteria in developing their rankings. Who can argue with a ranking system that examines college admission rates, incoming student GPAs and standardized test scores, and the success of alumni? Why should anyone fault organizations for ranking schools based on transparent criteria? Most importantly, if you can compare cars, doctors, and mechanics based on third-party rankings and ratings, then why should colleges be off-limits?

Finally, there is a fairness issue here. Colleges are asking parents today to contribute as much as $55,000 a year for an undergraduate program. It goes without saying that this is one of the most important financial investments a family will make. As a consumer, you are entitled to as much information as possible when it comes to making this important investment decision. We happen to think that it is outrageous that any college would demonize a ranking system that provides parents with another tool to help narrow down their kid's college list.

We certainly don't believe that rankings should be the be-all and end-all of how you choose your colleges. Those choices depend on a lot of different criteria that are unique to every family. Rankings can and do have limitations, as we've discussed elsewhere in the book. But we strongly advocate that parents arm themselves with as much information as possible, and we do think the rankings have an important place to play in your college search.

Applying like a Pro

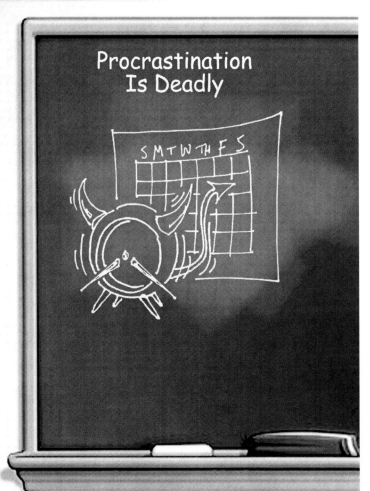

Procrastination is Deadly

> Take-away:
> *"Procrastination makes easy things hard, hard things harder." – Mason Cooley*

A sure-fire way to turn the college search process into a living nightmare for everyone is to procrastinate. In fact, a guaranteed way for college-bound students to put obstacles in front of themselves in a self-destructive manner is to procrastinate. You either pay now or pay later with interest. As Christopher Parker said, "Procrastination is like a credit card: it's a lot of fun until you get the bill."

Does your teen put things off that he or she should be focusing on in favor of something enjoyable or familiar? Is your child actively looking for distractions from the college essay that needs to be written? Perfect examples of procrastination are checking e-mails constantly or sitting down to start the college essay and then grabbing something to eat immediately after sitting down.

If you are noticing symptoms of procrastination, the first question to ask yourself is whether this is uncharacteristic of how your kid typically acts, or is it consistent with the way he or she usually operates. Knowing why your kid is procrastinating helps you figure out what to do about it. The goal is to diagnose the issue so that you can help your teen accomplish what needs to be done. The goal is not to do it for your kid or to coerce him or her into doing it to the point that it is about you not them. It's about them learning to be accountable and taking ownership of the next phase of their lives.

Here are some of the reasons for procrastination that you should look for in your kid so you can help them prevent the negative consequences of not getting the college applications done sooner rather than later.

- *Fear of failure*: What if I don't get in? I will let myself and others down. Better not to try.
- *Indecisiveness*: An inability to make decisions leads to a lot of time spent on thinking about what to do with little or no actual results.
- *Perfectionism*: Some kids are perfectionists, so they don't get it done because they are constantly working to make tasks perfect in their eyes.
- *Disorganization*: An inability to organize, prioritize, and schedule work leads to piles of paper and a big heap of somewhat finished work.
- *Distractibility*: Just having an environment filled with other things can distract a kid – think senioritis big time!
- *Avoidance*: The process can be perceived as boring and unpleasant so kids may avoid it for more attractive alternatives like friends and videogames or just about anything else, including yard work.
- *Complexity*: Remember, your kid has not gone through this before, so it can seem overwhelmingly complex with a lot to keep track of and the stakes seem high. If your child is one of the first to go to college in your family, it can seem even more overwhelming.

Do any or all of these symptoms exist in your household? Once you figure out what is holding your child back, you can identify ways of helping them. You know your kids better than anyone, so have confidence. If needed, get help from others, such as a high school college counselor or independent college consultant, to lead you through the process and track your kid's progress.

Regardless of what you try to do to encourage and push and prod your kid, remember to try to keep it positive. In order for change to occur, you have to engage your kid's mind and heart. Just talking to your kid and giving him or her all the rational, logical reasons for getting the tasks of the college application process done will not work. You need to engage your kid's heart as well because this is a very emotional time.

Try to get them to appreciate the fact that this is about their future and that you are working with them, not against them. They need to realize that all the hard work they have put in can be wasted in a matter of months if they don't focus. A high GPA, great test scores, and all the hours spent on activities can be wasted if the application is perceived as sloppy, incomplete, and impersonal. Plan ahead to ensure smooth sailing through the application process!

Aa Bb Cc Dd Ee Ff G
Do As Much As Possible
To Make The
Application Look Good
PLAN "A"

Do As Much As Possible To Make the Application Look Good

Take-away:
The devil is in the details.

College-bound students need to recognize that the college application process and the application itself are part of the continuing journey toward adulthood. It's really like their first resume and not unlike the job search they will experience after they are done with college. They need to realize that the college application is their opportunity to differentiate themselves and to make a positive first impression about who they are, what they have done, why they should be admitted, and what they will contribute to the campus community.

There are a lot of specific aids for beefing up an application from a detail standpoint, so we won't cover that here. Do a Google search on terms such as *improving college application* and *making college application better* and you will find a lot of helpful insights on the mechanics. We'd like to focus instead on the mindset that students and families should have when approaching the application process, and more specifically, the four corners of the application.

Get your kid to approach the application from the standpoint of someone else reading it. Ask your kid to read their application and answer these two questions: (1) What would you think of yourself? and (2) Would you admit yourself to this particular college based on what you read?

A common business concept that applies to the college application and to the entire college admissions process for that matter is the *elevator pitch*. The elevator pitch requires that a person be prepared to deliver a compelling case for their idea in the time that it takes to ride an elevator, or between thirty seconds and two minutes. Think of the college application as your kid's chance to tell their story.

What is your kid's story and what would he or she want to highlight for the college admissions staff if they had a very short period of time? Well guess what, the common application and supplemental information is your kid's version of the elevator pitch in the written word. Your kid's application will be among thousands of applications in a big stack at the college. Many applicants will boast as many or more activities and awards as your teen.

So what makes your kid stand out? First, ferociously focus on the details. It starts with the little things. If all applicants have superior credentials, how will admissions staff view your student if the application is incomplete, poorly written, and/or includes typos? Standing out with sloppiness and errors is a recipe for disaster! After taking care of the basics, it's really concentrating on creating an image of your student that best represents them. Focus on quality over quantity. Be determined to create a holistic, cohesive picture of what your student has to offer and deliver the message in a concise manner. Engage the readers so that they feel like they know your teen and really want to meet them. The application should leave the reader picturing the student on campus and contributing to the life of the campus.

Stay true to your high schooler and don't encourage him or her to sell a false picture, but highlight his or her strengths. Creating the elevator pitch will serve your student well in the college admissions process but will also build your student's confidence about what they have achieved and what they have to offer when they are admitted. It's the process of forecasting the story of your student's college life.

What's Your Plan B (and C)?

Take-away:
*Break down your list into thirds, with a third reach, a
third comfortable admits, and a third safety.*

We have a friend who was an incredible student in college. He racked up nearly straight A's, was elected to the student council, chosen by faculty to be Phi Beta Kappa, and seemingly set on the fast-track to academic success. His enthusiasm led him to apply to law school, as many top students do in their senior year of college. In this case, our friend's way of picking law schools was rather suspect – he simply applied to the top ten law schools in the United States. He had no backups. He was certain that he would get into at least one of the schools, and quite frankly expected to get into all of them.

What did he do in the year following his senior year of college?

He worked as a bank teller.

He was rejected by every single law school on his list. This is a true story.

This illustrates the worst-case scenario – choosing so many highly selective schools that you allow for the possibility of getting rejected by every institution on your college list. We're not going to sugarcoat this; if this happens to your teen, it will be a catastrophe. If all your kid receives in April are denial letters, he or she will almost certainly have to go to a community college because no other institution will take your kid that late in their senior year of high school. You can forget about your kid going away to college and starting all those dreams of making new friends, taking cool courses, and starting a new life. Instead, he or she will be forced to sit out one year at a four-year college because of a tragic mistake of overconfidence. The good news is that this doesn't have to happen to anyone and *is 100% preventable.*

We believe that every student, even those with sky-high GPAs and superb SAT or ACT scores need to bulletproof themselves. We advocate a "one-third, one-third, one-third" strategy. One third of their selected schools should be colleges that are ubercompetitive institutions – in other words, the schools that they have a slight chance of getting into but where the odds of admission are fairly slim. Such schools would almost always include, for example, Harvard, Stanford, and Yale. Don't feel bad about classifying these as reach schools – they are long-shots for every single student in the United States.

The next third should be schools that are in the comfort zone. These would be colleges that, based upon the average test scores and average GPAs of incoming freshmen, fall squarely within the acceptance guideposts. Think of these as schools where your teen would be very surprised if they were denied admission. All colleges should be able to provide you with average GPAs and test scores of incoming students, by the way.

Here's the most important part. Regardless of how well your kid has done in high school, a full one-third of the schools should be safety schools. Before we go any further, let's implode one myth right now. A safety school does *not* mean extremely low-ranked institutions that you would never think about your kid attending. Rather, a safety school means a college where their scores and GPA are on the high-end of the average incoming students. It also means that these are schools where if they were forced to attend they would not only be perfectly happy academically, but would also still benefit from an academic pedigree that could get them admitted to top graduate schools. There are many such schools in America that have high acceptance rates not because they're terrible institutions but perhaps they're located in a somewhat undesirable part of the United States. Some schools, like University of Redlands in California, are "diamonds in the rough" that are undiscovered gems of higher education and have generous acceptance rates.

The most important thing to do is to enter the college admissions season with a battle plan. Your college planning should always have a clear Plan B and Plan C just in case your kid winds up receiving a lot of denial letters in April. Although it is cliché, it does bear repeating: you always hope for the best, but prepare for the worst.

Just don't have your teen be the student that winds up spending a year as a bank teller because his hubris led him down the wrong path.

Essays

Essays

Take-away:
Get personal and passionate.

Think of all the things that your kid has absolutely no control over when it comes to the college application.

Their transcript is set in stone, and they can't change grades they have already received.

They can't write their own letters of recommendation (or at least we hope they don't!).

As far as activities go, they've either participated in something or they haven't.

And if they've read this far, they already know that we feel strongly that there is very little that a student can do to dramatically affect his or her SAT or ACT test scores.

But the one part of the application that a student has complete control over is the essay. In fact, the essay is the greatest mechanism that any student has to differentiate him or herself from everyone else. The most important thing to realize is that especially at competitive colleges and universities, the essay usually becomes the deciding factor between similarly situated students.

Although it seems obvious, many students seem to forget what a personal essay is all about: YOU! When you're asked to write a personal essay you need to emphasize the personal, intimate, and revealing. We've been consistently struck by how many students never actually write about themselves in their personal essay. Instead, in an attempt to wow the admissions committee with their intellect, they choose to talk about their views on current events, or perhaps their favorite book, or a movie they've recently seen. After you finish reading these types of "personal" essays, you really don't understand anything about the student that isn't on the application itself.

When you write a personal essay you want to think of it as sitting down for a college admissions interview. Because you don't get to interview in most cases with a college admissions official, the personal essay becomes the interview. You want that essay to illustrate your values, goals, and passions. The essay should express in words the essence of who you are. The essay serves as your opportunity to create a personal experience with application readers that gets them excited about you as a person and leaves them with a picture of you being part of their college community.

Another major problem we see with students is that they forget their audience. You can't blame students for writing their college admissions essays as if they're writing their AP English Literature exam or submitting a paper to their History class instructor. That's what students do all academic year. But students need to think of who the essay will be read by – a college admissions official. These officials will read literally hundreds of essays over the application period. They will not have a chance to meet the student personally. The last thing they want to do is to be bored, or to read a regurgitation of things that are already on the application. Your essay should touch upon things that are unique and create linkages between what the student is all about and what the school has to offer.

One final but important point. Never ever send off your personal essay without having everyone you know provide you with honest feedback. What we have learned over the years is that it doesn't matter who reads your essay – if you have a compelling story to tell, people from different political, religious, or cultural backgrounds will all usually find the essay to be engaging. On the other hand, we've also seen the opposite – that when the essay is poorly written and communicates little if anything about the student, then virtually everyone who reads the essay will tell you it was tedious (if they're being honest with you). Therefore, before you send off your essay, make sure that your firewall – in other words, your friends, family, and teachers – have all had a chance to provide input so that errors are caught before the essay ever sees the light of day in a college admissions office.

Deadlines

Take-away:
"A goal is a dream with a deadline" – Napoleon Hill

Setting deadlines is a critically important part of a successful college search. The thrill or stress of cramming is not the recommended path for your college-bound teenager or the rest of your family.

Set your college application deadline for Thanksgiving of your teen's senior year. Why ruin their holidays during their final year of high school? Besides preserving your family's last holiday season for fun and relaxation, the Thanksgiving deadline has the other advantage of providing a significant cushion for the unexpected. It also means that the people who are writing your student's recommendations will have a lot of time to write a stellar personalized letter and thankfully allows them to enjoy their holidays as well.

Starting with the end date in mind, here are some tips on how your child can stay on track with the college search and application process so they can meet deadlines.

- Start with the end date and go backwards when writing down what needs to get done.
- Always leave a cushion or buffer for when things need to be done and plan for the unexpected.

- Find a time and place for your child to focus on what needs to be done and avoid distractions.
- Find ways of rewarding progress so your teen will continue to make progress.
- Find a way for your child to be held accountable. This is where having another student, guidance counselor, or private counselor can be very useful.
- Break down the task into easy, digestible chunks to avoid being overwhelmed and see if there are things that you can do to help.
- Get them to start right away so that they don't get overwhelmed.

The goal is to create a concrete plan that has a lot of flexibility built in so that ultimately your kid can get the job done well and with the least amount of the stress and anxiety associated with the process. Remember that there will always be unexpected problems and surprises that need to be addressed. It's normal and shouldn't throw you off course since you have sound planning and buffers. With deadlines and a plan, teens can take care of everything that is in their control so that they have time and focus to take care of the many things out of their control that will come up. For example, a form that was not filled out or a recommendation that was never sent or received can be easily taken care of if the self-imposed deadline is a couple of months before the actual deadline.

Avoid the stress, anxiety, and yelling and screaming that typifies the average family's experience near college application deadlines. Set a self-imposed deadline ahead of the real deadline and stick to it (Thanksgiving, not January of senior year). Everyone will be happier.

The process will be less stressful and painful. The likelihood of a successful outcome will be much higher.

Recommendations

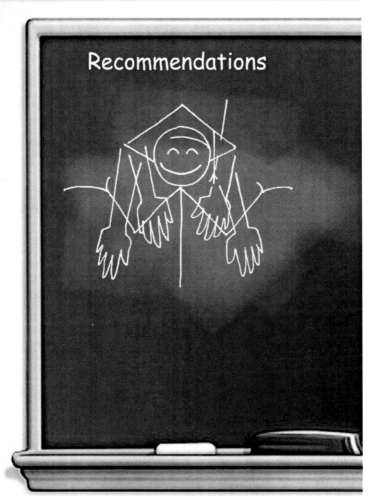

Recommendations

Take-away:
Secure commitments early from recommenders — even before the end of junior year.

Recommendation letters are often an afterthought in the college application process. On the surface, it seems so easy. How easy can it possibly get? You have a sheet of paper provided by the colleges, the student gives it to the teacher, and you simply wait a few weeks until the letter is done and submitted. Voila! You're all done. It seems incredibly simple.

However, with just a little time and strategy, you can do a much better job than this.

The two things that are the most important in the recommendation hunt are timing and selection. Let's take timing first. High school students should begin to identify recommenders as early as their sophomore year of high school. The student will want to identify two or three teachers who really "click" with them, who obviously give them high grades in their classes, and teachers with whom they can hopefully take multiple classes. This is important because when your teen asks for a recommendation letter, these teachers will have not just one class to draw anecdotes from, but rather multiple courses, and they can talk about your kid's academic success throughout the years.

Selection is vital as well. Many students simply think about the most popular teachers at their high school and ask those people for a letter of recommendation. However here's the problem: the more popular the teacher, the more students who will be asking for a letter from that same teacher. We believe that it doesn't matter how popular a teacher is – all that matters is that a teacher likes the student, respects his or her work in the classroom, and knows enough about the student to talk about him or her in depth in the letter of recommendation.

An ideal letter of recommendation not only talks about a student's academic accomplishments but also tells the committee about what drives a student, how that student compares against his or her peers, and also reflects upon that student's prospects for success in college. If a teacher only has the experience of one class with the student and knows little if anything about what the student does outside the classroom then they're asking exactly the *wrong* person to recommend them for colleges. Again, recommendations provide an admissions office an independent view of the applicant – what makes them tick, what makes them unique, and why they should attend the college.

Don't wait until the last minute. The quality of the letter of recommendation is directly proportional to how early the teacher is asked in the student's senior year of high school. If the student gives their teacher one or two weeks to do the letter and asks the poor teacher sometime in late October or November, they are going to get a letter that will probably be interchangeable with those of every other student at the high school. For all intents and purposes, that letter will do nothing to add to the kid's college application.

If your teen is applying to very selective schools, consider that the very best applicants have chosen their recommenders early in their senior year and will have cultivated those relationships all throughout high school.

We happen to think that letters of recommendation are a unique opportunity for forward-thinking students to really hit a home run. Your kid's classmates are waiting until the last minute and asking the wrong people, and in return they're getting blasé letters of recommendation.

Use their procrastination and laziness to your teen's advantage and ask the right people, cultivate the right relationships, and get a dynamic letter that truly adds value to the application.

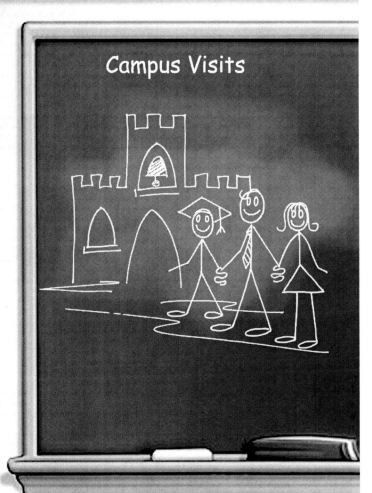

Campus Visits

Campus Visits

Take-away:

Seeing is believing: How a campus visit can help you sort through the many options.

Visiting college campuses during the college search process can be a very useful tool in the selection process. When it comes to exploring college campuses we recommend a staged approach.

For some assistance on the types of questions to ask on a campus visit, do a Google search for the term "college campus visit checklist." You will get a bunch of hits from reputable sources with how to plan for a visit, the things to look for, and questions to ask on a campus visit.

First, get a feel for what the college is like and what the campus looks like. Tour a college campus very early on in the process. In fact, we recommend visiting a local college way before the student's senior year. This gives teens a taste of what college is like without the stress of deciding. It also takes the mystery out of college and makes the whole process feel less intimidating. It doesn't even matter if the student is interested in the college. Go to the closest option possible just for the experience.

When the college search is in full swing, then we recommend doing research on the web and through guide books to get a sense of what factors matter to you and your family. Services such as http://www.campustours.com/default.aspx provide videotaped campus tours. Campus visits can be an expensive endeavor and the tours are often very similar and led by paid student employees who are marketing the college. Therefore, videotaped campus tours can be a cost-effective way of seeing the campus in the early stages of the search.

In the final phase, when specific schools have been selected and decisions are being made, a campus visit can be very helpful. The visit can serve two very important purposes: First, it is an opportunity to show the admissions staff that your student is serious about the college and an opportunity for the student to verbally give his or her elevator pitch about why they want to attend the college and what they have to offer. There is no better way to close the deal than to have a conversation with the admissions staff. It's their chance to make the application come alive in the minds of the people who read applications. Second, it is an opportunity for the student to *test drive* the college and picture themselves on campus. They can be the discriminating consumer and really ask themselves whether they would be happy on the campus for four years.

The campus visit should go beyond the campus tour and planned activities. Visit classes. Stay overnight. See what kids are doing outside the classroom and outside the planned activities. Ask a lot of questions and probe beyond the politically correct answers students give. The student should read between the lines and look for opportunities to have real experiences on campus that are outside of the marketing effort. What does their gut say about the college?

Make a lot of observations and engage in frank conversations to get a real sense of campus life. After all that investigation, have your kid ask him or herself, can I see myself here for the next four years? Why or why not?

Admissions Interviews

Take-away:
Admissions interviews are a good idea and an easy way to fortify your application. What you should expect, the pitfalls, and what you can do to help yourself.

Given the fact that the typical college receives thousands of applications every year, most colleges don't have the time or the personnel to interview most applicants. However, there is one way to talk directly to the college – by having an interview in your hometown. These are called alumni interviews, and they substitute for an interview that would ideally happen between an admissions official and the student on a college campus.

Relatively few students avail themselves by taking advantage of alumni interviews, which is a shame. This may be due to the fact that most high schools don't do a very good job in orienting students about how alumni interviews work, why colleges invest the time and money to set these up, and how students can ace the interview.

First of all, how exactly do you set up an alumni interview? There is no one process that applies to every college, but generally speaking this is how it works: The student needs to make contact with the admissions office, sometimes through the application, sometimes via the web, and occasionally via telephone. They express to the college an interest in an alumni interview and the college takes care of the rest. They'll locate one of their graduates in your area, and that alumni will contact the student to set up the interview. It's a very simple process. In fact, most of the work is done by the colleges.

Who are these alumni that get selected to conduct the interviews? Well, as you might imagine, these are people that are very proud of their college. Otherwise they wouldn't volunteer their time to do this. And they are volunteers – they are not paid one penny for conducting the interview. They come from all different occupational fields, and span every racial, gender, ethnic, and religious designation. In fact the only common denominator is that they really have a strong interest in helping students learn more about the college and in providing students with some information that they might not get from the college catalog.

Students are often curious as to where these interviews happen. That's also set up between the interviewer and the student. In general, these interviews are held at local coffee shops or at the place of business of the interviewer. It is fairly rare for the interviewer to meet the student at the student's home or at the student's high school. So be prepared to meet the interviewer in a public place.

Okay, so now we get to the really interesting part. What kind of questions will the interviewer ask? There are obvious questions the student needs to be ready for. These relate to why you are applying to that school, what things you might want to study, and background about your grades and your activities. *The student should assume the interviewer knows nothing about them besides the fact they are applying to the college.* One thing the interviewer will not ask the student in most cases is what other schools the student is applying to; if you are asked this, don't provide a direct answer because frankly that is none of the interviewer's business.

These interviews are important not only because they help the student to learn more about the college but also because in many cases the interviewer will write a report about the student that becomes part of the admissions file. The best way a student can be prepared for the interview is to dress appropriately, show up on time, and engage in a real conversation with the interviewer.

Your teen should be honest with the interviewer about any questions or concerns he or she might have about the college.

Be sure that your kid has done his or her homework beforehand and knows about the top programs, popular majors, and other special features of the college. Remember, your teen is having an interview not unlike one for a job.

Your child should also have a copy of the transcript and college application handy because the interviewer likely does not have this information and it will leave a lasting impression of professionalism and preparedness on your child's part.

The very best interviews between students and alumni are free-flowing conversations instead of a formal question-and-answer session. If the student leaves the interview feeling they gained newfound knowledge about the college and had a chance to ask many questions, then chances are they've hit a home run with the alumni interview.

The FAFSA:

What They Don't Tell You

Dealing With the Finances: How Does Your Primary Home Factor In?

> Take-away:
> *Figuring out what to do to pay for college is a complex issue!*

Paying for your kid's college while maintaining your own life is a complicated issue. When you look at the cost of higher education it can look impossible. Finding any possible legal loophole to protect your resources looks very attractive.

The FAFSA is used for determining federal aid. Your primary residence is not included as an asset and therefore is excluded from the calculation for financial aid and the EFC (estimated family contribution). On the other hand, over 600 colleges in the U.S. use the CSS Profile to determine non-governmental aid such as a college's own grants, loans, and scholarships for students. The CSS Profile uses a different methodology compared to the FAFSA and includes more specific questions, such as whether you own your primary residence and its value. Therefore, even though the FAFSA does not ask about the value of your home, the colleges may want to know this information.

Some people recommend that you pay down your mortgage on your primary residence to reduce your available liquid assets. There is a potential advantage to this approach; you are protecting your family assets and increasing your equity in your home. The potential downside of this approach is that you are taking a liquid asset (cash) and putting it into a non-liquid asset (your home). The danger of doing this is that if an unexpected event occurs, such as a job loss or a major health catastrophe, you might find your family in a bind because the money is locked up in the house. Financial experts recommend that you keep three to six months' worth of emergency funds available; you may be unable to do this if you pay off your mortgage.

Ultimately, you have to make a decision about what to do with the available liquid assets that you have. Besides your primary residence, there are really no other places where you can shelter your assets. The decision to put available liquid assets into your house or not represents a bigger issue that all families face, which is how to pay for college while at the same time maintaining your family's lifestyle and not putting yourself into a risky situation if your circumstances change.

There are no easy answers. It comes down to how your family balances its financial responsibility and your teen's individual financial responsibility for his or her education. It is a partnership and commitment on both parties' part and needs to be discussed so that everyone comes out of the college experience with preserved financial stability.

FAFSA: Fill It Out Regardless

Take-away:
Get in the front of the line for funds.

One of the most common complaints heard from millions of American families is that they make too much money to qualify for college financial aid. So why bother filling out the FAFSA? In their mind, the FAFSA will only yield free money for college if you are poor – whatever that means – and therefore it's embarrassing to even *think* about applying for financial aid.

High schools tend to reinforce this idea. How many of us have sat through the ubiquitous "FAFSA Night" at the high school auditorium, only to hear about how complicated the process is and about how the entire system is geared toward those with pressing financial need? Too many high schools associate the FAFSA with desperate financial circumstances, and many families that are homeowners, have stable jobs, and have even a semblance of college savings for their children feel as though the whole process is geared toward those who fall somewhere perilously close to the poverty line.

All this is pure hogwash. Fill out the FAFSA regardless of your financial situation.

The single worst decision you can make in the college application process is to not fill out the FAFSA. There are many reasons why you should fill this out, but perhaps no reason is as compelling as the fact that almost everyone who fills out the FAFSA gets *something*. Is every family guaranteed a generous scholarship? Of course not. It's entirely possible that you will fill the FAFSA out and not get any scholarships, grants, and fellowships. All you might be offered is a combination of federal, state, and private loans.

However, the worst-case scenario – you only receive loans – isn't so bad. Let's say, for example, your family has significant college savings, is paying down the mortgage, and has real assets. If you don't fill out the FAFSA you are going to have to either dip into your savings or take out college loans. Private college loans are virtually always more expensive than government loans because the government subsidizes an entire family of loan products. The problem is you won't even qualify for most government loans unless you complete the FAFSA.

So if you're going to take out a loan anyway, which is what the majority of families do, why not at least get a loan at the lowest possible interest rate?

And the news gets even better. College financial aid offices, contrary to popular perception, are not in the business of bankrupting American families. Under current methodologies employed by college financial aid offices, roughly 5% of a family's total net worth should be earmarked for a kid's college education. This really isn't as bad as most parents would've originally thought. Because of that, your expected family contribution for college might be significantly smaller than you anticipated. But here again, the college financial aid office will be totally unable to help you unless it has information about your financial situation. Just because your kid fills out an application for college does not mean that the school suddenly knows all about your financial portfolio. In fact, unless you complete the FAFSA, you don't really exist to the financial aid office.

Also keep in mind the realities of modern college education. There are thousands of private four-year colleges in the United States competing for students. Surprisingly, many charge roughly the same when you combine tuition, room and board, and other expenses. There is no baby boom generation coming through the pipeline right now, which means that these schools are actively competing for your teen. By not filling out the FAFSA, you don't give these schools the opportunity to compete for your teen on a financial aid basis.

Finally, we want to emphasize something that surprises many families. Although a lot of high schools make the FAFSA out to seem like solving the Rubik's Cube, it is actually a remarkably simple process. All you need to know is how much money you made the previous year, how much money you have in the bank, and that's about it. Most of the FAFSA is actually dedicated to biographical information, such as your age, Social Security number, and your level of education. They'll ask you if you participate in any government programs. It can all be done electronically, which is terrific because the government software actually catches mistakes as you're typing into the system. Rather than seeing this process as being cumbersome, the government has – shockingly – created a system that works pretty well and is fairly easy to use.

Completing the FAFSA doesn't cost you anything, it might yield you significant financial aid, and the worst-case scenario isn't so bad. So what are you waiting for? Fill out the FAFSA.

Do It On January 1. Period.

Take-away:
Start the year on a high note.

Happy New Year! January 1 is the day that the FAFSA sweepstakes starts. Get it done right away. Don't delay. However, don't try to fill it out prior to January 1 because that is not allowed.

Make the FAFSA deadline the first thing you have to do prior to getting ready for tax season. Thus, the first tax day becomes January 1. The second tax day becomes April 15.

Getting the FAFSA completed January 1 means that you will be in the front of the line when it comes to eligibility for federal, state, local, and college scholarships, grants, and loans. Waiting means you are further back in the line. Waiting until your taxes are done could mean that you will miss out on money to finance your education because the money runs out. We have found that the greatest mistake parents make in seeking financial aid, apart from never filling out the FAFSA, is waiting too long to fill out the FAFSA precisely because it does not prioritize their application for student aid.

On January 1, fill out the FAFSA to the best of your ability with the data you have. It is okay to estimate on the FAFSA and there is no penalty for doing so. You can always update and modify your FAFSA after you have submitted it, once your tax returns are completed.

Manage the entire FAFSA process online. Go to www.fafsa.ed.gov. In order to submit the FAFSA on January 1, you need to plan and coordinate with your teen.

Obtain your FAFSA personal identification number (PIN) for you (one of the parents) and your kid at www.pin.ed.gov. This speeds up the process because you can submit your FAFSA electronically once it is done; the alternative is to send in a paper signature page that slows things down and adds another step in the process. The bonus to the electronic application is that once you set this up you can use it for the next four years – and that thankfully makes the FAFSA process easier in subsequent years.

Collect your financial materials toward the end of the calendar year so you can do a very close financial estimate for the year. Items to collect include a pay stub from the end of the year (since you will probably not have a W-2 in early January), bank statements, mortgage statement for primary residence, mortgage statement from second property and land, stock, and retirement statements. The goal is to accurately report your financial status for the year so that the college can generate a Student Aid Report (SAR) that includes the expected family contribution (EFC). The nice thing about this process is that it actually sets you up for getting the documentation ready for your tax returns. In essence, filling out the FAFSA early makes tax time much easier as you near April 15.

Print out the FAFSA worksheet (available on the FAFSA website) during the holiday season between Thanksgiving and Christmas and write down your estimates in preparation for filling out the form. This will make filling out the actual FAFSA form easy on January 1.

Trust us. Fill out the form with the data and sign and submit the FAFSA with your student and your electronic pins. Print confirmation of when the form was submitted. If you do the simple steps above, come January 1 the FAFSA will be done in a flash and your family will be well on its way to making the college financial aid process a success. By filling out the form early, you will expand the universe of possible sources of financial aid because you are at the front of the line.

Colleges Are Not Looking to Bankrupt You (It's True!)

Take-away:

They expect about 5% of your net worth to go to your kid's college education.

Most parents are just plain cynical when it comes to college tuition. After all, who can really blame them?

A single year at a good private college or university with tuition, living expenses, and other incidentals, easily exceeds $50,000 a year. That's more than what the average American family makes in one year! The cost of college has risen much faster than the rate of inflation. In fact, most Americans collectively shake their heads and wonder why colleges cost so much. There are many reasons for that, and even experts are not entirely sure of all these reasons.

However, believe it or not there's more good news than bad news when it comes to how colleges approach helping families. Contrary to popular belief, colleges have absolutely no incentive to bankrupt the families who send kids in their direction. It doesn't make sense as a business strategy for the simple reason that graduates who are burdened by massive amounts of debt do not make for very happy alumni (translation: poor alumni don't make for very generous donors to the university).

In fact, financial aid offices can be your best friends in battling the high costs of a college education. Our universal experience has been that most financial aid officials are extremely understanding of the dire straits that families sometimes confront. The officers are not highly paid, they are generally overworked, and the one thing that keeps these people in the field is an abiding interest in helping families afford college. Forget about all the images you have of a college financial aid officer as a Wall Street hedge fund manager raking in massive amounts of money. The financial aid officer at a typical university is someone who is not making a huge amount of money and spends most of the year trying to crunch the numbers to make it possible for kids to go to college.

Here's the best news of all: based on current methodologies, colleges expect a 5% contribution of the family's net worth for one kid's college education. That means that even after four years of college, the average family can expect about 95% of their total net worth to remain intact.

There's even more good news: colleges have generally been increasing the amount of financial aid they are providing out of their endowment funds. For example, schools like Harvard and Yale are now guaranteeing 100% financial aid for certain classifications of students. State attorneys general around the United States are cracking down on colleges that are not distributing more of their endowment for financial aid reasons. All signs point to the fact that colleges are more aware than ever before that families need financial assistance.

Help!

Our strong advice to you is to not lock horns with the financial aid office. Don't take an aggressive posture with them because they're not your enemy. Everyone is really on the same team; the colleges desperately want your son or daughter to attend their school, and you want to make it financially possible.

We find that families who take a collaborative approach with the financial aid office, who ask probing questions and understand the realities of how colleges distribute funds are often those that are quite happy with the process. The worst way to approach this is to demonize the college financial aid office, treat financial aid officers in a demeaning or abusive fashion, and then expect that your kid will receive significant financial aid for college. They're your friends. Treat them as such.

Don't Put Assets in Junior's Name

Take-away:

Junior will be expected to contribute to college.

Let's be clear about one thing from the start; there really is no way to "game" the FAFSA. The FAFSA is not like your tax return, and there is no ten-volume tax code that applies to filling out the FAFSA. It is a very easy process that asks for very straightforward information. In fact, as we write this, the federal government is exploring ways to simplify the FAFSA even further!

We understand that parents are looking for ways to minimize their total net worth as it appears to college financial aid offices. We also know that for many parents, it is apprehension at its worst to wait to see what the colleges will offer to help pay for college. Add to this a large number of poorly-trained college financial planners that try to advise parents of ways to hide their assets on the FAFSA, and you have the recipe for a very explosive mix of disappointment and anxiety.

The worst piece of advice someone can give you regarding "gaming" the FAFSA is that you should shift your savings into your son or daughter's name. The thinking goes that if you do this, the parents will appear poorer – in other words, will have fewer savings – and therefore more financial aid will result. This is the furthest thing from the truth.

College financial aid offices will *always* expect a student to contribute most, if not all of his or her savings and work earnings to their college education. This obviously does not hold true for parents. As we mentioned in an earlier chapter, a very small percentage of a parent's total net worth will be expected to go to their teen's college education. So when you shift your savings into your son or daughter's name, you take money that would only partially be earmarked for college and instantly devote it almost entirely to your kid's college education. That cash for college will reduce any scholarships, fellowships, grants, or work-study assistance that would otherwise be provided to the family by the college.

There is another reason why you shouldn't do it. The FAFSA will ask parents how much they made the previous year. There's absolutely no legal way to hide your income in the FAFSA process. The second thing the FAFSA will ask for is your total savings. If you simply take those savings and place some or all in your son or daughter's name, you still have that asset showing on the FAFSA. That cash doesn't disappear, doesn't make you seem poorer, and you can't hide it. So why try?

Our view is to simply be honest throughout the FAFSA process. Don't play games by shifting money into the accounts of others, don't try to make yourself look poorer on paper, and whatever you do, don't lie. Many families don't know this, but the federal government actually requires college financial aid offices to audit a random percentage of FAFSA returns each year. Because they are completely random, *you* might ultimately be selected for a thorough audit to confirm all the financial information you put on the FAFSA.

If you're honest with the college financial aid office, you have nothing to worry about. However, if you succumb to the temptation to mislabel assets, earnings, and savings, and if you are one of those randomly selected for an audit, you can be virtually assured that your future financial aid offers from the college will be diminished or, at the very least, closely scrutinized.

College financial aid offices understand how expensive their institutions are, and you really don't need to go through the trouble or the risk of putting your assets in Junior's name.

It Gets Easier

It Gets Easier

Take-away:
After the first time, the FAFSA gets easier because you are not starting from scratch.

The FAFSA can seem like a difficult and painful form to fill out. It's like doing your taxes earlier than April 15 and then doing your taxes again. The FAFSA can also bring up broader issues for parents related to letting go of their high schooler and letting go of a lot of money. It can feel overwhelming, really scary, and like a slow, painful process that will last for four years.

We can't solve the broader issue of what you have to pay for college, but we can put you at ease about the actual process of filling out the FAFSA after the first time.

Once you get through the first year of filling out the FAFSA, the following years get much, much easier because information is pre-filled for you from the previous year's form. You will also be a veteran of the process, so you'll know what to expect.

The process of completing the FAFSA becomes an exercise of looking at what was in last year's form and updating it. What makes it particularly easy is that all the general information only has to be reviewed and modified only if there have been changes, such as an address change. In fact, Nelson completed the FAFSA for his two teens in less than ninety minutes.

So, as laborious as the first time filling out the FAFSA can seem, there is no excuse for not filling out the FAFSA every year because it gets easier. Filling out the FAFSA every January should be among your highest priorities because every year is a new opportunity to state your case for financial aid to the government and to the college. Don't miss out on the potential benefits that your child may receive by filling out the FAFSA.

So, go to it and don't forget to fill out the FAFSA come January 1.

Do It Electronically. Period.

> Take-away:
> *Electronic filing of the FAFSA has advantages. For one thing, you get help filling it out correctly!*

Remember the good old days of filling out forms on paper and hoping that your writing was legible and that you had filled out the form correctly and completely? What about the bottles of correction fluid for when you messed up? If there is one time when you should absolutely use the Internet to complete and submit a form, it is to fill out the FAFSA.

Why do the FAFSA online? It comes down to making your life easier and to getting the form done as quickly and accurately as possible.

Doing the FAFSA online means being able to speed up the process for eligibility for student aid because you and your kid can electronically fill out, sign, and submit the form rather than dealing with paper forms that you have to put in the snail mail. The turnaround time for getting your Student Aid Report (SAR) can be reduced by weeks in some cases because your paper signature doesn't have to travel all over the country and sit in a pile in someone's office.

Filling out the FAFSA online also means that you and your teen can complete the form when it is most convenient (of course this means

January 1, based on our recommendation, remember?) because with the online version you can save your application and come back to it. It's nice to know you don't have to have the whole thing done in one session.

In addition, doing the FAFSA online means access to online help; in fact, real-time, live help is available right on the website by clicking the "Need Help" and "Live Help" icons.

One of the best reasons for completing the FAFSA online is that it means automatic data entry and error checking. This eases the stress of filling out the FAFSA and reduces concerns of incorrectly filling out or missing any data entries. Online worksheets will crunch the numbers you entered and automatically calculate and enter some of the data for you. No math required! The built-in error-checking feature does immediate checking and flags errors that need to be corrected. The Sokens definitely appreciated the peace of mind of knowing that the form was done correctly before pressing the *Submit* button.

With all of these advantages, there is no reason not to electronically fill out the FAFSA. The only reason not to do it is if for some reason you don't have access to the Internet – in which case we would say go to your local library and use their free Internet.

Save time. Avoid costly mistakes. Reduce stress. Have peace of mind. Complete the FAFSA electronically.

Where Do We Find Money?
Starting Points

Scholarships: Five Things You Need to Know

Take-away:
Scholarships are not as hard to get as advertised, and many websites and books are useful.

Winning a scholarship is not only one of the most exhilarating experiences in life, but it is a meaningful way to reduce the overall burden of college tuition. However, the vast majority of kids have not been taught by their high schools – or by anyone else, for that matter – about how to apply and compete for scholarships.

There are five important rules when applying for scholarships that can help most students enormously when hunting for free money.

First, planning is everything. In fact, we will take a good planner over a high-scoring student any day. Our experience has been that a student who is a superb organizer but has a 3.5 GPA will usually do better with regard to scholarships than a completely disorganized 4.0 kid. Why? Because the disorganized student will wait until last minute to complete his application, will invariably exclude important pieces of his background that could help him in the scholarship hunt, and will turn in an inferior product that demonstrates little passion and even less proofreading. About 80% of winning a scholarship is knowing important deadlines, getting all the pieces in place well before that deadline, and ensuring that you have taken part in enough activities, volunteer opportunities, and other things in your life that make you interesting to the scholarship committees. You obviously can't do this if your application is due in one or two days.

Second, students need to write to the audience. They wouldn't apply for a Rotary scholarship the same way they would apply for a Greenpeace scholarship, because they are comprised of different members. Just because the student won't see the scholarship committee doesn't mean that he or she does not have an obligation to learn a little bit about the membership of the sponsoring organization. Understand who will be reading the scholarship application and *write to that audience*. The student shouldn't lie about his or her background or belief systems, but they should try to find what they have in common with the people who will be reading their application and who will make the final call about who wins the money and who does not.

Third, follow directions. If the scholarship form tells the student not to include supplements, don't do it. If they limit the student to a certain number of words, which is very common, don't have them push the limits of the committee's tolerance. We can tell you that many committees will simply disqualify the student if he or she does not stick to their word or page limits. The reason scholarship committees are strict about their rules is because they want to make sure that everyone competes on a level playing field. If one student is allowed to submit a lot of extra information, it would give him or her an unfair advantage.

Fourth, just as with applying for colleges, with scholarship competitions the essay is one of the most important documents that the student submits to the committee. Approximately 90% of the time spent on each scholarship application should be devoted to the essays. Again, because the student is writing to very specific audiences he or she does not want to create just one essay, photocopy it, and send it to all the scholarship committees. Students can certainly use pieces of one core essay for all their competitions, but ultimately they need to tailor each essay for the unique membership and the purposes of the scholarships they are applying for.

Finally, finding a scholarship opportunity has become remarkably easy given the explosion of Internet sites devoted to financial aid. Websites such as www.fastweb.com and www.finaid.com have become real workhorses for parents and students who are looking for scholarships. Here's the trick: students should register themselves with high-quality websites (we list some great ones in the Appendix) and let them send the student scholarship information when they find a new award that matches the student's background, interests, and qualifications. Students should also spend time with their college financial aid officer and with their high school counseling office to see what sort of small scholarships they are aware of that may not be advertised elsewhere. Remember, the fewer people who know about any given scholarship, the better the student's chances of winning it.

With a healthy dose of organization, planning, and preparation, students will be more competitive than the vast majority of kids seeking free money for college.

Loans

Loans

Take-away:
Loans are a way to finance education, but consider them carefully with a short- and long-term view.

Parents want to provide their kids with the best possible education so that they will be well-positioned for the future. With the soaring costs of higher education one of the financial issues that most families have to deal with is how to fund college and the role that student loans play in that equation. It's the balancing act between parent and student investment in their future.

Loans create immediate short- and long-term consequences for the student and his or her family that need to be discussed. In the short-term, loans can help bridge any gaps of funding that the family has and are attractive because payment of federal and state student loans are deferred until the student is out of school. So, the key short-term concern becomes, how much borrowing is required so that the student and parents can comfortably live their lives.

However, the long-term perspective that needs to be factored in is whether the student will be able to afford the monthly payments after graduation. According to a National Postsecondary Student Aid Study authored by Mark Kantrowitz, two-thirds of college students borrow to pay for college, and their average debt load by the time they graduate is $23,186. That translates into a monthly payment of $266.83 for ten years at 6.8%. So, the key question in the long-term is, can the student handle the payments after college based on their expected starting salary? This is particularly important if the current economic environment forces graduates to compete for scarce jobs, accept lower-paying jobs, or pursue jobs outside their career field. A further caution is that federal student loans and some private student loans will not be forgiven in the event of bankruptcy.

If your student needs to take out loans to fund college, here are some tips. Always take advantage of federal and state student loans first, as they have the best terms and easiest process for applying and repayment. With recent legislative changes in the student loan program, private banks no longer serve as the middlemen with federal loans. Loans are managed directly by the federal government, which will likely reduce borrowing costs for families.

Don't immediately trust a list of preferred lenders that the college provides because there are no uniform criteria by which institutions select lenders. In fact, in some cases the institution may be getting payments or benefits from the lender, so do some digging before selecting a lender.

Private student loans through banks and other financial institutions will almost always require the student to get a co-signer who has a high credit score. As a parent, the thing to consider is that by co-signing the loan with your kid, you are taking on responsibility for the loan if your teen is unable to pay the loan back. How they manage loan repayment will affect your kid's and your credit rating. So, co-signing on a private loan is a long-term commitment.

A college investment is still a very good investment, but it is important to consider the role of loans so that the student does not start off in life in a precarious position. Ultimately, students should strive to find work where their passions lie without the stresses of student loan debt hanging over their heads. The student needs to realize that at some point they will have to take responsibility for repayment of the loan and that an investment can turn into a major financial liability if not managed well. Furthermore, in the case of a private loan, you as a parent are taking on long-term financial responsibility along with your kid if they get into financial trouble after graduation.

Before taking out loans, it is critical to have a frank discussion with your child about what they are doing now and plan to do post-graduation. They need to realize the financial responsibility they are taking on!

Federal Work Study

Federal Work-Study

Take-away:
Federal Work-Study is a relatively easy way to pay for basic living expenses in college.

When students receive their financial aid award letters in April of their high school senior year, a common component is a Federal Work-Study award (sometimes called "FWS"). There is quite a bit of confusion about what this program is all about, but in a nutshell it is one of the easiest ways for students to defray the costs of college while being a full-time student.

Perhaps the best way to explain work-study is to discuss what FWS is not. First, a federal work-study grant is not a guarantee that a kid has a job waiting for him or her on a college campus. A work-study award simply gives a student the right to *find* a work-study job. This is actually important because students without financial need are prohibited from applying for work-study positions on campus.

Here's how it works: The federal government provides most colleges and universities with funding to allow students with financial need to work on campus while still maintaining their role as full-time students. Because these jobs are subsidized by the federal government, colleges can utilize students in a variety of roles from everything from the library to the gym to dormitories. We think this is a win-win situation;

students can earn a little bit of income while in school, while the colleges are able to staff their departments in a relatively low-cost way. We also happen to think that work-study is one of the best programs out there. There are a lot of reasons for this. First of all, most FWS jobs are pretty easy. A typical FWS job might involve shelving books in the library or checking IDs at the gymnasium. There are very few work-study jobs that require strenuous effort. We also like the fact that FWS positions are on campus, which means that the student's boss is someone in higher education who understands that students need to take time off for important papers and examinations. In fact, a lot of colleges and universities require supervisors to give students time off should they need extra time for their class work.

Unfortunately, there is one downside to these positions: pay. As you might imagine, there can be a big difference between the pay of a work-study job and what a student might find off-campus. On-campus employment generally pays about the minimum wage or a bit higher. Many students could earn more money per hour working off-campus. But off-campus employers are certainly not going to be sympathetic to students who need time off for their studies, and the time and effort it takes to get to off-campus jobs usually negates any additional income that would be received by the student.

If your kid is granted a federal work-study award, consider yourself lucky. Not only is your student eligible for a low-effort on-campus job while going to school, but they might even build partnerships with important professors and administrators that will serve them well not only in college but after graduation. But do be prepared; our advice is to arrive on campus and immediately have your teen find out where the job postings are for the work-study program. Your kid will usually need to provide supervisors with a resume, and he or she might have to interview for the job. But if your kid is diligent about this, a work-study job can be secured within the first few weeks of arriving on campus.

As with everything else in college life, those who arrive prepared are those who often snag the very best FWS jobs on campus. If a student waits too long, chances are that he or she will be stuck in what might be the very worst on-campus job imaginable: the cafeteria. That is a job where they will exert quite a bit of energy!

Housing

Take-away:
Freshmen are often required to live on campus their first year, and then they are free to live wherever they want. Balance savings from off-campus living with the convenience of on-campus dorming.

Next to tuition, housing is the single biggest cost of your kid's college education. It is a serious subject – but one that curiously often gets overlooked. Many parents think that there are very limited options involving housing; either you live on campus or off campus, or if you go to a local school you can live at home and commute to classes. But there are actually quite a few choices, and we have strong views about how to explore your options.

If your kid is going away to school, they're probably going to live on campus and will likely be required to by the school. This only makes sense because you don't want your kid to spend their first few weeks at college looking for a place to live. It's also good news because colleges are investing millions of dollars to update and improve their dormitory facilities, and there are a wide range of housing options, from substance free dorms, to single-sex dorms. This is a very positive development in higher education.

Then the choices get a bit tricky. The default housing arrangement

252

for incoming students is a double room. They will be paired up with a roommate who the college thinks, based upon questionnaires filled out by incoming students, would be a good match for them. It goes without saying that there is a bit of luck involved here. Very few roommate pairings work out perfectly. If the college gives freshmen the option to have a single room – and not all colleges do – you will pay a hefty premium for that privilege. The upside, of course, is that you don't have to worry about your kid getting a roommate that is incompatible. They simply won't have a roommate. If they're the type of student that prefers to study alone with minimal distractions, this may be worth the premium you pay.

After your kid's first year of college, they're typically free to go off campus or to remain in the dormitories. Whether this makes sense financially depends almost entirely upon where the college is located. If you go to college at Columbia University in New York City or the University of California at Berkeley, then your kid will pay a substantial (gut-wrenching?) premium to live off campus because of the high cost of living in New York and Berkeley. On the other hand, if your kid is going to school in a rural area, it will quite likely be cheaper for them to move off campus. We do not think that your kid should base their decision of where to attend college upon the cost of living in the area. However, do keep in mind that the housing costs will drop dramatically if they attend a school in a low-cost area, such as colleges in the South or the Midwest.

Let's focus a little bit more on the issue of roommates. Many students immediately see roommates as a way to slice their housing bills by half, and there is obvious financial merit to that argument.

However, our experience has been that the more roommates that live under one roof, the more distractions that confront the student. If you believe that students are in college to credential themselves for graduate school – as we do – then you want to keep the distractions at a minimum. If your kid has a very sociable personality and tends to be easily distracted in the company of others, we would strongly recommend that they reconsider taking on one or two roommates. If you can do it, consider investing the money in a single room so the student can focus more on studies.

One last thing that many parents don't realize – there is a way to have the universities pay for the student's housing completely. After your first year of college, your kid might be eligible to become what is known as a Resident Advisor, or "RA." This is an upperclassman that lives in the dorms and essentially manages a floor full of underclassmen. Their responsibilities range from counseling students to ensuring safety and cleanliness and to simply being the eyes and ears of the university during the academic year in the dormitory. This is one of the few on-campus jobs that pay substantial money because it wipes out the housing costs. However, this does involve a huge amount of time and energy on the part of the upperclassman, and it's absolutely not a job for everyone. The student needs to have extreme discipline in separating their academic life from their personal life. They must be able to juggle the demands of working with underclassmen that are adjusting to college while at the same time maintaining their laser-like focus on academics. It's a very difficult juggling act, but it can be the perfect way to say goodbye to one of the heftiest price tags attached to a college education.

School: Follow the Money

Take-away:
Follow the money and look at the institution's coffers, first and foremost. It's where it all begins.

There are a lot of great colleges that also provide great long-term value because of the education that they provide. Therefore, one of the first places to look for financial aid are colleges that provide a superior experience at a reasonable price tag.

Some institutions initially seem financially out of reach based on the sticker price; however, rarely does anyone pay full price. Some colleges and universities such as Harvard, MIT, Stanford, and University of California schools (think Berkeley and UCLA) have committed to reducing student educational debt by limiting student loans in financial aid packages (www.ProjectOnStudentDebt.org). For a listing of the endowments of institutions in the U.S. go to http://www.nacubo.org/. For example, as of 2009 Harvard had the largest endowment in the U.S. and Canada at $25.66 billion.

Another way to look at the cost of college is to calculate the net cost of college after all the "free money" is factored in so you can get a true picture of what each year is going to cost you. If circumstances have changed in your household and/or there is a school that you really like that did not offer you as much aid as another school, we suggest you to call or write a letter to see if they can increase your aid.

Be a savvy consumer and work hard at getting the best deal possible. Also, look at the long-term value of the education your child will receive, taking into account the quality of the education and the opportunities he or she will have. Weigh these factors to come to a final decision.

Final Thoughts for Families

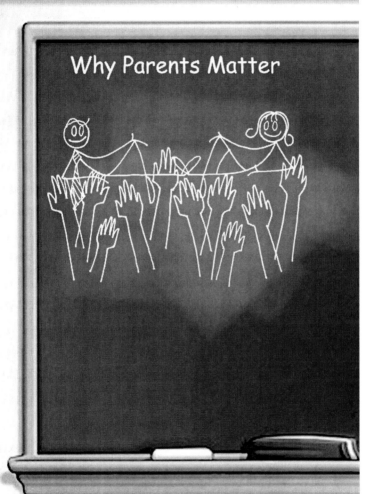

Why Parents Matter

Take-away:
Hang in there and kids will be better off. Even if sometimes they don't seem to appreciate your help, they do.

Both of us are parents and were college students in the not-so-distant past, so we can say with a great deal of confidence that when kids go to college it creates intense emotions on both sides. The kids are incredibly excited to begin a new phase in their life even if they are a bit worried about all the new people and classes that they are going to encounter. Chances are they'll be moving to a new city – another point of excitement and perhaps some healthy anxiety.

And for parents, the emotional roller coaster could not be greater. It's probably the first time that your kid has left your house for an extended period of time in seventeen years. You're going to look at your dinner table each night and notice that strangely vacant chair where your son or daughter used to sit. The strangest thing of all? The once hyperkinetic activity going on in your house is going to subside to something approaching normalcy.

Then comes the tough part – how to parent after your kid goes to college.

Parents of college kids tend to be either overly involved with their kids' lives or tend to be too detached. As with all things, we counsel moderation. We also think that it's important to understand how we define supportive parenting during the college years. First of all, understand that this is a letting go process. As hard as it is to come to grips with, your kid will probably never return home permanently. Your teen has truly begun the next phase of life – one of real independence in a new world where they will make decisions on their own. They will often succeed, and sometimes fail, but as any parent knows, that is simply part of the learning process. Being a continuous safety net and bailing your kid out of every problem they get into (read: sending them more and more money) is certainly not a way to help a college student develop independence, maturity, and responsibility.

We happen to think that parents can play an important role in their kid's college success by providing them with tremendous encouragement to not only study hard but also to step out of their comfort zone. Taking classes in subjects that they know nothing about; doing a study abroad program to an interesting but little-understood part of the world; joining clubs with arcane and bizarre names that attract eclectic members – that's what college is all about. It's about growing professionally and personally, exposing themselves to new ideas, opportunities, and people, and most importantly, finding out more about themselves. It is important for students to graduate with skills that they can market to employers. But we also like to think of college as perhaps the only four years in someone's life when they can truly immerse themselves totally in subjects and classes that don't necessarily have any direct application to the working world. And that's a good thing.

We've talked to many other parents and have sat through our share of graduations. One thing that has always impressed us is the genuine joy of a parent at graduation. You can see it in their eyes – the glowing pride of a proud parent in the audience watching their child receive their diploma. For the student receiving a degree, it is recognition of their hard work over four years.

A parent should also recognize that the degree also means that you've done your job superbly. You provided your son or daughter with the breathing space they needed to accomplish what they wanted in college and explore new areas. You ideally gave your kid a passport to adventures in another part of the country and perhaps even an opportunity to study abroad. And most importantly, you've given your son or daughter a potentially new and refreshing outlook that might forever change how they see work, life, and people.

Parents do matter. They matter because they can provide students with much-needed encouragement during the college years. But let students find their path on their own and don't be their constant safety net. Rather, be their biggest cheerleader that they can always depend on for encouragement as they go through the college years.

Communication is Vital

> Take-away:
> *Focus on communication and building your relationship.*
> *It's another opportunity for you to be a parent.*

We are finishing our journey together. As parents you have a major role in your kid's next phase of life. Your guidance and leadership are critical. It will take patience. It will take perseverance. It will take understanding and encouragement. And more than anything else, it will take open, honest, and loving communication between all family members. Recognize that kids are early in their development and don't know what the future holds, so you need to play the role of a guide and leader. Give yourself a break and don't be hard on yourself when you mess up or get ticked off. Don't take things personally, as well. Trust us, it is worth it in the end and you and your family will survive.

Partnership is critical and in fact required for a successful college search. It requires open communication. Being a leader and guide as a parent requires being an adult and setting up the right environment and atmosphere in your family that enables open communication. This requires planning before conversations even happen. Some tips:

- *What are the landmines?* Identify the landmine topics and activities that cause stress and emotional tension and figure out ahead of time how you will deal with them and when you should talk about them. Some items on our list are completion of applications, finances, FAFSA, college selection, and just tracking what needs to be done and whether it is done.

- *Are you creating a self-fulfilling prophecy situation?* Prepare yourself by not assuming too much about how it is going to go, where it should go, or what your student's motivations and intentions are. Examples are going into a situation with thoughts like: "Talking about getting the application will end up with Johnny saying he has been busy"; "Mary needs to obviously know that we can't afford that college"; "Fred always procrastinates and is avoiding what he needs done on purpose, as always."

- *Don't go into it with emotion and negative assumptions.* Assume the best of your kid and try to understand their situation. Extinguish negativism when you have to talk about difficult things. Step in the shoes of your kid and identify what they know and don't know. Use each other to vent about things that bug you and also give each other feedback before and after you have conversations.

- *It's ultimately about getting to a goal and building your relationship.* Make it okay for your kid to say what they think and feel. Give them time to express their point of view before cutting them off. In some ways, think about how you deal with colleagues at work and give your teen that level of respect. They are almost grown-ups.

Always remember that you are the parent! It's not unlike managing and leading people at work or in other organizations. You are the leader and you need to inspire your kid to follow you and accept feedback. You also need to be willing to get feedback as well. It is a partnership between you and your kid.

Ingredients For A Successful Parent In The College Application Process

Ingredients for a Successful Parent in the College Application Process

> Take-away:
> *It's time for you to stop reading and to start doing.*

We have provided you our insights and views on how to create the atmosphere for a successful college search. We've given you advice on how to view the search, what your role is, and where the pitfalls lie. Now it's your turn.

You have the ingredients to create your own recipe for success. We have talked about how you need to shift your perspective from being a manager to being a leader. Another picture to keep in mind is that you are transitioning from being the pilot that is in control to being the co-pilot that assists but does not co-opt the college selection process. You are the one that helps manage and even alleviate stress rather than creating or adding stress for your college-bound teenager. You are the guide or elder that provides a long-term perspective about what to consider and what works or doesn't work based on your experience and wisdom. You are the advisor that helps the kid see the dangers of debt and the beauty of a well-designed academic program.

So, are you ready? A few parting words of advice to keep in mind that we covered in the book and that we leave you with are:

- Remember, you are the adult(s) and will need to set the tone for the family, as this is scary and unknown territory for your teen. Even if there is an exterior of calm, confidence, and even aloofness, there is anxiety going on under the surface.
- Open communication and managing emotions are critical.
- Don't get sucked into negative patterns of thoughts and behaviors that lead to fights, but rather focus on the prize and your kid's future success.
- Doing the research and knowing what you know and what you don't know are critical in helping your child.
- The college search has changed since you were there, but there are a lot of options and a lot of resources to help you through it if you seek them out.
- Take on your fears and address them by being open with each other and, again, do your research and seek advice.
- Create a family atmosphere that generates positive energy and grows your relationships rather than causes stress and frustration.
- Organization, planning, scheduling, and delegation can make the process less painful and stressful.
- There are a lot of college options that fit your student's and family's needs, and it's a matter of sorting through the choices.
- The application and financial aid process does not have to be scary if you plan ahead.
- Tackling the money issue is manageable if you work together as a family.

Parents have a major role in leading the family and your child through this major rite of passage. You have the opportunity to help your teen successfully navigate this next phase of his or her life.

In the Appendix, we provide two perspectives from the Soken kids, who reflect on their college search and first year college experience. We also provide a section of resources that we believe will help you as you jump into your own college search.

Good luck with your journey!

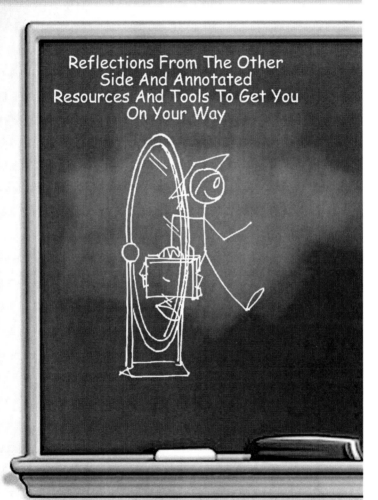

Reflections From The Other Side And Annotated Resources And Tools To Get You On Your Way

Appendix A: Emmaline and Evan's Perspectives

Contributor: Emmaline Soken
Sophomore, Macalester College

So the time is coming to apply to college, and you're knee-deep in paperwork – you have your information brochures, your common app, your letters of recommendation buried in there somewhere. It's pretty overwhelming. However, it's important to remember you're not alone and it's important to stay as organized as possible. Here are some general tips right off the bat:

General Tip 1: Communicate with other students applying to college and older college students.

Find out what other students are doing in their college search. You may find that a lot of them are just as clueless (or even more so) than you are, and so aren't much help. But it can be a comforting thought to know you're not alone in this confusion. Also, talk to students who have already been through it. See? It didn't kill them, so it won't kill you. Listen to them regale you with tales of their search and what they wish they would have done or not done. If for some inexplicable reason, you can't find anyone who is willing to share their stories, try looking online for tips. You can also talk to your parents about their college experience, but understand that the college search for them was probably very different and so not everything will apply to you. Just remember to be patient and respectful; don't disregard everything they say because they're "old." If nothing else, talking to them will assure you that the college search won't kill you.

General Tip 2: For organizational purposes, keep each college together.

Remember what you have done for each college so you don't get your Harvard mixed up with your University of Texas and start sending colleges the wrong applications. A good way is to get some folders and label them each with the college name. Even if everything is done online, write yourself a handy to-do list and stick that in the folder. Your parents will probably be concerned about this aspect of the college search, and you might be annoyed by their over-attentiveness. Remain calm and understand that they are just as nervous as you are about this process; like you, they don't want you to lose something important or miss a deadline.

General Tip 3: Send in your applications well before the deadline to avoid scrambling.

Now I understand you all will be busy with end-of-the-year papers, projects, and tests, but that's no excuse to do things at the last minute. Just think of the application process as a high-priority homework assignment, and if you get your applications in with some time to spare, that saves you that last minute scrambling if there's a piece missing and you have twenty-four hours to get it in and a final at eight o'clock the next morning. Doing extra work earlier will save you stress later. There is the potential for tension to build up between you and your parents. Your parents might be constantly asking or reminding you to get your work done, and it can be exasperating. However, remain calm and understand their perspective; they are just as concerned as you are about college, but they don't have the control. Be sure to assure your parents that you have everything in hand and prove it to them by being careful and diligent with the application process.

A big part of the stress related to the college search is that mysterious looming fear known as The Great Unknown. There are endless unknowns, some more looming than others: What if I bomb a college final? Will my professors like me? What will my room look like? What kinds of people will be there? What's the food like? A lot of these unknowns can be made known by a simple college visit, but even if you've done all your research and spent two nights at a prospective students' weekend, there's a lot you won't know until you're actually attending a school. Having just finished my first year at college, perhaps I can speak to some of these fears and assure you everything will turn out fine.

Fear #1: What if I don't make any friends?

Lucky for you readers, I was probably one of the least social people on my campus, and I STILL managed to make friends, so I can most firmly assure you that no matter how unusual you might be, you WILL find people who like you for you. You meet people in classes, in your dorms, in your activities, etc. Unless you actively try NOT to make friends, it will happen pretty naturally.

Fear #2: What if the classes are too hard?

Colleges understand that every student is on a different academic level and so provide ways to help them succeed. Remember, the professors and college staff are not your enemies; they aren't coming up with insane classes and assignments designed to destroy your soul. They WANT you to do well. That's why colleges have introductory-type classes to ease the transition. In fact, most of the time students are surprised by how easy one of those introductory courses is. However, later on if a class or assignment is particularly challenging, be active about getting help. All colleges have some sort of tutoring or academic service where students can get help. Also, keep a clear perspective – you can't ace everything. Do your best, and if your best happens to be a C, that's just fine.

Fear #3: What if my professor hates me?

First of all, if you try to steal, cheat, and lie your way through school, yes, your professor might very well hate you, but if you're just nervous to ask questions or go up to your professor's office for fear they will be annoyed, rest easy. Again, professors aren't out to get you, they're out to educate you; that's why they do what they do. Sure, there will be some professors who you don't get along with. In fact, I've had a good amount of tension between a professor and myself, but it's not the end of the world, and no, they do not hate you. They probably don't have TIME to hate any of their students. Look at it as a learning experience. If it's a problem, just finish the class strong and then don't take the professor again.

Fear #4: What if I keep getting lost and miss my classes?

Oddly enough, I believe this was my greatest fear. Nothing made me more nervous than desperately searching strange hall after hall, glancing at my watch in a panic and having people think I'm an idiot. Have no fear. This never actually happened to me, and if a class is so well hidden that you really simply cannot find it, you probably aren't the only one and you can lean on your fellow *losties*. At most schools, the departments are grouped relatively close together. Usually all humanities classes are in one general area, and then the sciences in another. Rarely will you have to run all around campus within the space of four hours, trying to find where everything is, but again, if you do, no doubt you aren't alone.

I know there are many other fears besides these four, but I can give you a three-word reply to all of them: **You aren't alone.** There are other students in your position and there are services that can help you. Whether it's a medical need, a navigation need, an academic need, or anything else, there will be someone who can help you. Now, I don't expect all your fears to just melt away after reading this – fear is a natural response to something we're unsure about – but hopefully you can allow your brain to take control of those quivering emotions and be confident that those fears will eventually go away.

Having gone through the college process and my freshman year, there are some things I wish I would have done a little differently that I think could be useful to you.

1. I wish I had visited more college classes.

Before I go any further, I have to emphasize the importance of visiting schools. DO IT. However, I caution against just visiting during those specially-designed prospective student days. They change things for those days, even the quality of the food. The most useful thing, I believe, is going to the school when it's in session and visiting the classes. That's why you're going to college; you don't go for the food or the dorms or anything else, you're going in order to get an education, and if you don't visit a class, you really will have no idea what it's actually like to attend the school. Sure, you have those brochures and all, but they only say good things about everything. Go and experience it yourself.

2. I wish I had been more organized.

You may think you're only going to go through the college search process once, but, like me, you might decide to transfer. After deciding on a college, I essentially threw everything around in piles (never throw anything AWAY) and left it. When I went back to start applying to other schools, I had to dig up a lot of old papers and try to remember things I hadn't looked at in a year. Spend some time getting organized now, because you don't know what you might need in the future.

3. I wish I had visited more schools.

This isn't something I personally wish for since I visited a fair amount of schools, but it's very common for college students, especially those who don't like their current schools. When you only visit one school, you have nothing to compare it to. You have no idea what other opportunities there might be, and if you do start having doubts halfway through the year, you will definitely begin to wonder what shade of green the grass is over that college fence, and that is not a pleasant state to be in. If possible, visit at least three schools so when you do make your choice, you can rest easy knowing that you are making a well-informed decision.

Lastly, here is a list of miscellaneous things my first year of college has taught me:

Lesson #1: If you don't get involved in activities within the first two months of school, you probably won't at all that year. College clubs and activities are some of the best places to make friends, so if it's something you want to do, do it as soon as possible. Now, don't go crazy. You will have schoolwork to do. It's a wonderful thing to cultivate other interests, but limit yourself to two or three extracurricular activities, depending on the time commitment. Sports, for example, take up a lot of time.

Lesson #2: Exercise is a great stress reliever.
What's the best thing to do when you find yourself overwhelmed by school and life in general? Eat? Watch TV? Wrong! Go for a walk, run, downhill ski, etc. Don't believe me? Just do a Google search on stress and exercise and I believe the result speaks for itself.

Lesson #3: Beware the Freshman 15.
Don't believe the studies that say this is a myth. It is not. If you're not an independently active person or in sports, college food is the

worst thing for your body. It's not even that the food is necessarily all bad – it's that you will have so many other options besides that salad bar, and knowing the minds of most people, they will go for the pasta or the double hamburger. I'm not saying you can never eat any of those things, but if you want to be conscious of your weight gain at school, pay attention to your diet and exercise.

Lesson #4: Getting work done early is awesome.

Now this wasn't especially awesome for me because I was the only one of my friends who would do this, so I would be lonely when I finished my work. However, if more people did this, there would be a surprising amount of time for fun. When you get an assignment, be thinking about it, prepping for it, and then just sit down and work on it. This might take some training, since so many people are procrastinators, but honestly, would you rather be up until three in the morning writing a paper, or up until three hanging with your pals?

Lesson #5: Listen when your professor is talking, especially at the beginning and end of class.

This seems like a no-brainer, but it's at these particular times that the mind starts to wander, and unfortunately, it's also when the professor gives the most important information. It's when he or she tells you if a deadline has changed, where to find something you will need for the class or assignment, and if a class period is cancelled or moved. You will want to know these things, because if you do not, it is painfully obvious to the professor and to the entire class that you were not listening. It can also affect your grade, especially if you miss your professor saying on a Friday that the deadline of that big project has been moved to Monday instead of Tuesday.

Lesson #6: Communicate with your parents.

Your parents will probably miss you when you're at college. They could see the fears in your eyes when you left and will worry. Even if it's just an e-mail every week, remember to communicate how you are doing when you're at school. Also, be prepared for new challenges while you're at school and when you visit home, as your relationship with your parents will be changing. Remember to try to see things from their perspective. Like you, your parents have their own list of fears. Do your best to assure them those fears can be put to rest.

Contributor: Evan Soken
Sophomore, Macalester College

The college search isn't too far behind me, and, in retrospect, these are some things that I wish I had been told. Luckily, you are being told by me. Let me break it down for you, beginning with the application process.

Application Process Tips:

• <u>Cast your net widely</u>: When you're sitting down at the beginning of the college search process and wondering what schools you'll even apply to, have an open mind. Believe it or not, Twitter, Facebook, and Pandora are not the *only* worthwhile Internet destinations. Browse a ton of college websites and just get a sense of what's out there. Check out schools of all sizes, locations, and reputations. A huge benefit of proceeding this way is that you start to get a framework of things you like as well as things you aren't so enthused about. It's great to have these reference points when you start to shorten the list of applications you are submitting.

- <u>Take a few notes</u>: You'll be taking a lot of notes throughout college so you might as well get some practice. As you embark on the Internet journey recommended above, take some notes; it's nothing color-coded or cross-referenced, just some basics like what you liked and what you didn't. Not only will these brief notes be helpful when you're narrowing the number of schools you'll be applying to, but it's also a great fact sheet when you are writing your "Why I Want to Attend Your School" essays.

- <u>Visit! Visit! Visit!</u> As the little header of this tip implies, I feel really strongly that PFs (prospective freshmen) should visit as many schools as they can. I am a campus tour guide at my college and I hear all the time about the difference that a tour or overnight stay can make. Visiting a campus keeps you firmly rooted in reality. It's easy to idealize a school and make it out to be the pinnacle of higher education – the perfect place for you. Visit. If it turns out to be *both* the pinnacle of higher education and the perfect place for you, great! But if it is *not* all you thought and dreamed it would be, it's better to find that out before you get on campus the fall of your freshmen year. On the other hand, sometimes it's easy to eliminate a school because of an assumption you have or a rumor you've heard – "That school is way too politically liberal/conservative for me," "It's way too big/small," etc. Again: *visit*. Find out for sure. Perhaps there is a wide diversity of political opinions on campus but the college has a reputation from years ago or you heard a story based on one person's experience. Maybe the school doesn't feel as big in person or maybe a small school has a lot of opportunities that make up for its size.

- Close to home as a benefit? Many of you probably feel the need to escape your hometown, spread your wings and soar into a brave new world. I know because initially I *only* looked at schools in faraway states with the dream that I would strike out on my own in a totally new place. In my particular situation, my sister and I were going to school at the same time, and it wasn't a financially clever thing to live a five-hour plane trip from home. As it turns out, in my desperation to fly as far from the nest as possible, I had missed some incredible schools in my home state. I found the college I currently attend only forty minutes from my house. It had everything I was looking for and more. There are things you can do to make sure that you have a separate experience and stay independent, even if you stay local.

On Campus Tips:

- Be bold. Get involved: As my wise sister already noted, it's pivotal that you get involved right off the bat. I'm repeating this one because I think it's so important – get involved right away. A lot of schools host involvement or student organization fairs during orientation to give the freshmen an idea of what that college offers. Be sure to go. Sign up for mailing lists, talk to the organization reps, go to a bunch of first-meetings, because it's always easier to drop the activities you're less interested in than to add more mid-semester/mid-year when everyone has already become friends or is in the middle of projects. Be a go-getter, be a pioneer, be an over-committer, and then be a smart person when you filter out all but your favorite activities. It's a great way to make friends and connections right off the bat and also to do something more than study. Realize that *everyone* is new and is trying to get to know people.

- Don't get discouraged: I know all about this. It's so easy, once the orientation euphoria wears off, to suddenly realize that you're on a campus and in a city or state where you know few people, if any. I enrolled at my college knowing that no one I knew would be in my class or be currently attending that school. I sat in my dorm at the end of the first week and thought about how I had only a few half-formed friendships to my name. Don't worry about it, guys. Seriously, it's week one and more people are feeling like that than you would expect. Just keep making efforts to be involved and meet people. The comfort level, the friends, and the fun will come with time.

- Make friends with upperclassmen: I realize that at some institutions this might be more difficult. But student clubs/organizations are great places to network with people outside of your class. Benefits? Well, probably they would make really awesome friends, but also they've "been there and done that" when it comes to your particular school, so ask them about what professors are good and for tricks and tips about class registration and paperwork. This has been invaluable to me, and it's so comforting to talk to someone who's an experienced student and knows what they're talking about.

Parent Tips:

- <u>Let us fail</u>. I know that for parents, it's a difficult thing to let their kids fail or to see them frustrated and disappointed; however, in this process it is imperative that you let your kids do as much as possible. It might be tempting to oversee every step of the process, but start to give the student more and more freedom. For example, let them do a college visit on their own and have them make phone calls or send emails to the financial aid/admissions offices. College is a time for us to start testing the waters of the real world on our own and seeing if we can make it, so letting us strike out on our own in small ways helps us build self-confidence as well as practical skills. Admittedly, mistakes will be made and deadlines will be nearly missed, but kids will ask for help if they need it.

- <u>Let your kids ask the questions important to them</u>. I know you are wiser and more experienced than your kids in the ways of the world, but let your kids ask the questions on a tour or to an admissions counselor. There are some things that may not seem relevant or important to you but are of interest to the student. I completely understand that maybe you have questions about grad school stats or financial aid or medical school acceptance, etc., but keep those questions in check until you're sure your student had all *their* questions answered. Another quick tip: don't remind your kid of a question in front of a tour guide or counselor. For example, "Sweetheart, remember to ask about financial aid." I'm sure you mean well, but I have seen enough looks of total mortification to understand that students would rather you just ask the question as opposed to reminding them as if they were a three-year-old who forgot to say "thank you."

- <u>Remind. They'll love you, then they'll hate you – but remind</u>. Even as you give over much of the work to your student, remember that you are also a guiding, experienced hand in this process as well. Teens, being the hormonal and generally bipolar creatures that we are, will sometimes be on top of things and resent parents' reminders as hovering and distrust. However, other times we will be caught up in the moment of high school commitments and forget about that financial aid form or scholarship application. It is at times like these when your student will love you for your benevolent, overseeing eyes. So be patient, be consistent, and it will all be over soon enough.

Appendix B: Recommended Readings

Preface:

There has been explosive growth in the number of books available regarding college admissions and scholarships, but we think that only a handful are worth your time and money. These books are among the best overviews of the college process and are well worth placing on your bookshelf.

College Gold by Mark Kantrowitz (2006)
ISBN: 0061129585

We have waded through many books on financial aid, but most don't reveal anything you couldn't figure out on your own. This is the exception. The very best book out there regarding paying for college is *College Gold*. It is actually hard to find this in a bookstore, but it can be ordered easily on Amazon or other online bookstores. The author, Mark Kantrowitz, is the creator of fastweb.com and is one of the best authorities on college financial aid in the United States. This book has quite a bit of detail regarding how colleges review your financial information, and after finishing this book you will be thoroughly familiar not only with the process of applying for financial aid but also in understanding how financial aid is divvied out to successful candidates.

Countdown to College: 21 'To Do' Lists for High School by Valerie Pierce with Cheryl Rilly (2009 second edition)

ISBN: 978-0-9656086-8-8

Getting down to the practical task of managing the college search and admissions process can be a challenge. It can sometimes be tough just to know where to start and to keep track of deadlines and due dates. This book, written by a mother of a college student, has practical "To Do" lists of what needs to happen during the high school years in preparation for college admissions. We found this book to be an easy-to-use guide for navigating the process.

Fiske Countdown to College by Edward Fiske (2009)

ISBN: 1402218974

This is a relatively new addition to the Fiske collection of college "how to" books, and it is one that we highly recommend. The book includes forty-one checklists that apply to every year of high school. What we really enjoy about this book is that it is clearly written and can be digested quickly – it doesn't waste your time. Even though it is a small book, it contains germane information about the college application process. This is one of the best of this growing category of college material.

Fiske Guide to Colleges by Edward Fiske (2011)

(NOTE: it is updated every year)

ISBN: 1402209614

If there is one book that is on the bookshelf of every college counselor in the United States, it is the *Fiske Guide*. And for good reason. We love the *Fiske Guide* because the authors travel to college campuses and talk to students and administrators to give you an unvarnished and "no holds barred" discussion about the pluses and minuses of each of the hundreds of colleges they select for review. We also have found through our visits and experiences with many colleges that the *Fiske Guide* largely makes accurate observations about the colleges it covers. We think you could easily save hundreds or thousands of dollars in campus visits by simply purchasing this book and reading the Fiske review of what life is like at the colleges you select. Yes, it's that good.

The Five-Year Party by Craig Brandon (2010)
ISBN: 1935251805

This is probably the most provocative recommendation on our list (hey, we love different viewpoints!). The author argues that American colleges have fallen far off the track of providing students with a top-notch education, and gives a very troubling overview of the pitfalls that can confront students who do not maximize educational opportunities while at college. Many of the scenarios – students taking five or more years to graduate, excessive partying, etc. – have become disturbing features at many American universities. Although we don't agree that many colleges have "given up" on teaching, as the author suggests, families should read this book to understand just how a lack of seriousness and focus can derail educational planning.

The Gatekeepers by Jacques Steinberg (2003)
ISBN: 0142003085

The author, a regular contributor to the *New York Times*, provides a rare behind-the-scenes view of how admissions offices operate at America's top universities. Although the book does not specifically give you guidance about how to apply to any one school, students would be well advised to understand the general process that governs how admissions offices operate. This is a virtual must-read for students who are applying to Ivy League-type schools because it helps readers understand just what works and what doesn't work in crafting a top-notch college application.

Going Broke by Degree by Richard Vedder (2004)
ISBN: 0844741973

This is another book that is fascinating reading because it discusses why college costs so much. The author gives you a well-researched and superbly-argued narrative in terms of why the cost of college keeps escalating. It's a great read and it provides parents and students with an overview of just how their tuition dollars are spent at America's colleges and universities.

Appendix C: Terrific Websites for College Admissions and Scholarships

Web Resources

Students today have a happy problem: too much information on the Web about college and scholarships. Rather than trying to navigate as many websites as you can, we recommend a focused strategy that mines several quality websites for information. Most importantly, register with these websites so that you can receive updates on college admissions news and scholarship opportunities.

College Admissions:

*   http://www.collegeanswer.com/index.jsp: This is another very good general guide to the college admissions maze, and it also includes good resources for scholarship hunting. This would probably not be a primary portal for college information, but it would be a wonderful addition to any of the other websites on this list.

*   http://collegeprowler.com/: What sets this website apart from others is that it's written by students of the colleges that are covered. Especially for those of you who are not planning to physically visit the colleges you are applying to, this may be a great way to get a good overview of the college from a student perspective. **Note**:

there is a subscription fee, but it is fairly minor. Many students find that the small subscription fee is worth it for this website.

- http://collegesearch.collegeboard.com/search/index.jsp: This website is from the College Board, which is one of the nation's leading authorities on all things college and is the publisher of the SAT. Here you will find a wealth of information including testing dates, admission requirements, and all sorts of other data that will help you make a good decision about where to apply to college. This is kept up-to-date and is among the most reliable websites for college searches available in the United States.

- http://www.gocollege.com/: This is an excellent general guide to all aspects of making the transition to college life. Apart from covering the transition to college, you will also find information regarding scholarships and financial aid, as well as advice about how to make sound choices once you arrive at your college campus.

- http://www.studentsreview.com: This is another website that relies on students to provide information about the lifestyle and quality of academic institutions. We are big believers that you learn most about what it is really like to be a student at college by reading what current students are saying about the institution. Keep in mind that the postings from students who fill out surveys about the colleges may not represent the entire student body, but you will at least get a sense of what issues the colleges face and the relative strengths and weaknesses of the institutions.

Scholarships & Financial Aid:

*   http://www.fastweb.com: This is perhaps the most popular scholarship website in America. Still free to students, this database purportedly contains billions of dollars in funding opportunities. The downside is that the sheer popularity of the website means that there are very few "hidden" opportunities here.

*   http://www.finaid.org: This website is a rich treasure trove of scholarship information, and well worth any student's time who is trying to locate college funding and other information about institutions of higher learning. We especially like the financial aid calculators that help you to guesstimate your expected family contribution.

*   http://www.fundsnetservices.com: Wonderfully categorized! Clicking the "Scholarships" link provides additional college funding sources.

*   http://www.grantsnet.org: This website bills itself as a "one-stop resource to find funds for training in the sciences." As the name implies, it is a clearinghouse for grant information.

- http://www.usnews.com/usnews/edu/dollars/dshome.htm:
  Best known for its school rankings issue, U.S. News & World
  Report's website is one of the best resources for learning more
  about institutions of higher learning and about strategies to find
  funding for higher education.

- http://www.wiredscholar.com: This goes far beyond mere
  scholarship information, covering everything from tuition
  waivers, internships, and other opportunities to defray the costs
  of higher education.

About the Authors

Jason Lum is president and founder of ScholarEdge College Consulting. He is the recipient of $250,000 in scholarship winnings, and has worked with hundreds of families, high schools, and universities as a college admissions and scholarship consultant. Lum is one of America's leading presenters on college admissions and financial aid, and has been profiled on CNBC, CBS News and Radio, and many national newspapers. He has a BA from Washington University in St. Louis, an MPP from Harvard, and a JD from UC Berkeley, as well as a College Counseling Certificate from UCLA.

Please visit www.scholaredge.com for more information.

Dr. Nelson Soken is a parent of two college students and his family's journey through the college search process was the inspiration for this book. He has a BA from Macalester College in St. Paul and a doctorate in child psychology from the University of Minnesota. Dr. Soken is a manager at Medtronic, Inc., senior associate with Barnes and Conti, Inc., and co-author of a book on innovation entitled "Lead the Pack: Sparking innovation that drives customers wild".

CPSIA information can be obtained at www.ICGtesting.com
Printed in the USA
BVOW010451130412

287599BV00006B/2/P